Praise for *Cross Addicted*

Liz R.—Trauma survivor

"Paula, thank you for sharing yourself! I ⸱ ⸱⸱ ⸱⸱ in church and was abused by two different pastors at two different times in my life and wondered what was wrong with me. I never understood that the pastors were wrong. It's been forty-five years now and I am finally believing what is true about me as God's dearly beloved child. I want the church to get your message of truth about trauma. I will continue to work on healing with my therapist and work on helping church leaders understand better who they are shepherding. #metoo and #churchtoo was a real trigger for me to do the work of healing and to help others see they too can heal. Thank you for your vulnerability."

Tonier Cain—founder and CEO of Healing Neen, Inc, a nonprofit, a Trauma Informed Care Expert, author of *Healing Neen*, and TV show host at the *Talk with Neen* Show

"I had the privilege and honor to interview Paula on my radio show. As a trauma survivor and former addict, I know the impact these issues can have on one's life. Paula's story is one of hope and overcoming many obstacles in life. Her book will point you to the one who can heal you and set you free, who is Jesus Christ. I strongly feel her book will help many whose lives have been affected by addiction and trauma."

Lorilee Craker—*New York Times* bestselling author of fifteen books

"I believe trauma may be the greatest mission field of the 21st century, and the most misunderstood issue of our day. The world is filled with traumatized people, desperately searching for answers on how to get free from their pain, trauma, and addiction. Paula's two-fold plan—surrendering to Jesus *and* working hard at recovery—offers a healing, hopeful path to recovery for those who are hurting and traumatized. It also gives church leaders a dynamic, essential, and beneficial tool for truly helping—not hurting—those in their care who are affected by trauma and addiction."

Brenda L. Yoder—LMHC, counselor, educator, speaker, advocate, and author of *Fledge: Launching Your Kids Without Losing Your Mind*

"Paula's heart in sharing her experiences is to help church leaders, family members, and those working with trauma survivors to best care for and love those affected by trauma. As a therapist and former school counselor and teacher who worked with multiple kids with trauma, I appreciate how she takes the reader to understand the world of youth when they are most often seen only by their behavior. This book is not only helpful for adult survivors of childhood trauma, but for anyone working with kids from hard places."

Dawn Scott Damon—pastor, speaker, and author

"Thirty-eight percent of all children will experience trauma. Some will never recover. Paula should have been that one. From a childhood of intense trauma, laced with neglect, extreme abuse, addiction, teenage pregnancy, and violence, Paula was debilitated in every normal function of development. To say she is a miracle is not an over-statement. Only a Supreme Being could piece together the shattered psychology of this broken young woman. In *Cross-Addicted*, Paula writes with tearful and raw emotion, giving us an inside glimpse of her pain while holding out a candle of hope for other survivors."

Andrea Blickley—Executive Director of The Lighthouse for Teen Moms; https://lighthouseforteenmoms.org

"I am one of the founders and the Executive Director of The Lighthouse for Teen Moms. In our Ministry, we often have young moms who come to us who have, in their young lives, experienced tremendous trauma. As a speaker, Paula has spoken truth into our girl's lives. In Paula's book *Cross Addicted*, she shares her story, but also takes you through a process of healing straight from His Word. She asks her readers important questions, that if answered honestly, will lead to real, deep, soothing healing.

"If you are an educator and want to better understand trauma and how it effects your students, read this book. If you are a ministry leader and want to understand those you minister to who are under the influence of addiction, or have other trauma in their lives, read this book. If you are someone who is struggling with trauma caused by addiction, neglect, or abuse, read this book!"

LoriJo Schepers—Executive Director of Barnabas Ministries, Inc.
"Paula Jauch speaks with a powerful blend of truth, heart, grit, and grace. Her story of triumph over tragedy, becoming victorious after having been a victim, gives power and inspiration to all who hear her speak and read her story. Her honesty and vulnerability provide safe passage for others to open up about their own heartache, while always pointing to Jesus Christ as the ultimate healer of hearts."

Pam Steele—elementary school teacher
"As an educator, I found it insightful to hear from a true trauma survivor. Paula Jauch brings a face to childhood trauma and shares how it affected every area of her life. She delivers an important message to educators about a topic that can sometimes be overlooked or misunderstood. Trauma can affect a child's learning, behavior, and relationships. It is important for educators to understand the role trauma can play in a child's everyday life. Paula's story brings awareness and hope for children who have suffered trauma."

Kristen Stieffel—writing coach and author
"Paula Jauch shows an astonishing amount of vulnerability as she opens her life story for readers to examine. It's a life full of trauma, abuse, and addiction. Her life is now full of recovery and triumph. Paula knows that this kind of example is needed to help other trauma sufferers toward hope. With blistering authenticity, Paula shows others the way with a heartfelt sense that because she's been through the ordeal, she can guide you through it as well."

Amy Majeski—Spectrum health nurse
"I had the privilege to hear Paula speak at one of her events ... Oh ... My ... truthful words have never been so beautifully delivered. As a survivor of trauma and addiction and a nurse who sees the effects every day, I needed to hear her message and encouragement. I promise you ... these words will challenge and encourage you wherever you are in your life journey. I strongly feel her book will help many people."

Pat Ackerman—trauma survivor

"I lived a life of feeling alone, that I was not good enough and that I did everything wrong, which came from my life of physical and emotional abuse. My journey to freedom led me to Paula. Her understanding of my pain through her past experience and her steps to healing helped loosen the hold my upbringing had on me."

Sue DeBoer—mentor

"When you have lost the love of a father and mother so steeped in their bondage to addiction, you have an orphan heart. I have seen Paula's heart rise out of the ashes into new life. Her Heavenly Father has restored her true identity, emotions, and health. I have been privileged to walk with her as a mentor watching all God has restored to her."

Cat Jenkins—spiritual mother and sponsor through Paula's recovery program

"I met Paula almost 20 years ago. I will never forget our first meeting. The person I met then has grown into a beautiful, spiritual woman. Now I hardly recognize the person she was and rejoice for the person she has become. I watched her heal and grow into who she was meant to be. She was already enough because she was God's child. Seeing her discover that and continuing to share her journey with others has been a precious gift to me and many others. This book will touch the lives of many."

Susan Etts—friend, wife, mother, and prayer warrior

"Paula's honesty and courage to share her story was a help to me in so many ways. Knowing that others have gone through similar things and have come out on the other side has given me hope for my future. Your message is needed, and it encouraged me to share my story one day. There are so many people who feel so lost and alone. And you make them feel like they are not alone after all."

Cross Addicted

Breaking Free From Family Trauma and Addiction

FOREWORD BY DAN SEABORN, FOUNDER, WINNING AT HOME

PAULA JAUCH

Cross Addicted

Breaking Free From Family Trauma and Addiction

REDEMPTION PRESS

Author photo by Josie Kamstra

Published by Redemption Press, PO Box 427, Enumclaw, WA 98022.

Toll-Free (844) 2REDEEM (273-3336)

Redemption Press is honored to present this title in partnership with the author. The views expressed or implied in this work are those of the author. Redemption Press provides our imprint seal representing design excellence, creative content, and high-quality production.

ISBN 13: 978-1-64645-144-9 (Paperback)
978-1-64645-147-0 (ePub)
978-1-64645-148-7 (Mobi)

Library of Congress Catalog Card Number: 2020902123

dedication

To the fatherless and the motherless who are searching to be free from the trauma of abandonment and rejection. My prayer is that you will know Jesus as a healer and get to know your Heavenly Father as a father.

"Father to the fatherless, defender of widows—
this is God, whose dwelling is holy.
God places the lonely in families;
he sets the prisoners free and gives them joy"
(Psalm 68:5-6 NLT).

Table of contents

foreword

Dan Seaborn
Founder, Winning At Home, Inc.

Any effort to help other individuals find their true identity in the God who made them is something I consider powerful and challenging. My personal story, like Paula's, has had many dark days. For years those dark days defined me. In the past few years, thanks to God's provision in my life, I have found a healthier path. As I read through Paula's book, I find correlations in our paths.

I believe for you, too, there will be encouragement and enlightenment for your life journey. The ultimate goal of life is to use our gifts to honor God. In order to do that, we have to be healthy. Sometimes doing what is healthiest for us can almost appear selfish, but let me remind you that Jesus himself took time to care for his needs. For those of you who think Christ did not experience the same types of hurts and emotions we do, I encourage you to take another look at the Gospels.

Jesus' life was full of pain, shame, betrayal, and brokenness. In fact, He is referred to as the Man of Sorrows. Just as Christ overcame those obstacles, we can also overcome. He knew when He was healthy His words would be healthy to others. I believe you will find Paula's book helpful in this process.

acknowledgments

Before I began to write my acknowledgments, I searched Google about how to write an acknowledgment. Even though I already knew what I wanted to write and who I wanted to thank, I am the person who still has to double check—okay triple check—everything. That's just who I am. Here's what I found on my Google search: What to write in an acknowledgment … "Many have asked this question. An acknowledgment should provide the author's statement that declares something to be factual, true, valuable, or appreciated, or in the end instance genuine."

So there it is, to be thankful and genuine. That is all I needed to read, and that is what I want to do in this acknowledgment and throughout my book. When I was in school I could never write one stinking paper because I was illiterate and nothing would stick with me, even when my teachers would try to help me. I was filled with too much trauma to learn anything. It's not that I didn't want to learn but my brain was in fight-or-flight mode, and I was just trying to survive. I spent my educational years being misplaced in many classrooms until I was in high school and I was sent to an alternative education school. I believe at this point my teachers and the educational system had given up on me.

I know this is supposed to be an acknowledgment thanking everyone who helped me write my book, but I felt you needed a little background into why I am so grateful to everyone who helped me along this journey.

First, I would like to thank Jesus my Savior for rescuing me from a dark pit and not allowing me to take my life. Thank you for whispering to my soul the words, "I want you to start sharing your story to help others and write a book." I argued with him about the book for a while. I had too much self-doubt to even think of writing a book, but with His help, I finished the task.

God brought many people into my path to get the job done. And though I still struggle with self-doubt and probably always will, I am learning to not allow these feelings to stop me from living out the will of God for my life.

Second, I would like to thank my husband Jeff, who loved me into wholeness. When we first got married seven years ago, I had not even tapped into working on my trauma and suppressed childhood memories. He continued to encourage me to get the help I needed so I could help others one day. When I would scream and kick and want to give up on writing this book and my healing, he would say with a gentle tone, "you know that this is what God wants you to do, and it will help many people one day." You are my forever man, and I want to thank you for your unconditional love and stability that you bring into my life.

To my four strong, beautiful children who God created with unique gifting. Thank you for allowing me to parent you out of my brokenness and thank you for being patient as I walked through my healing journey. One of my goals to finish this book was to show you that you can do anything you put your mind to if you don't give up. God has an amazing plan for all of your lives!

My spiritual mom, whose name is Carol Jenkins, but better known as Cat to me. Where would I be without you? When I walked into my first recovery meeting, I was suicidal and you came up to me after the meeting and said, "Why don't you give me a call." I am so grateful I did. The rest is history. You are the mom I felt like I never had and you cheered me on in so many seasons and one was to complete this book. Thank you from the bottom of my heart for loving me and believing in me.

Sue DeBoer, my friend, my mentor, and another mother figure. It's hard to look at you as a mother figure because you act and dress younger than me. Thank you for allowing me to lie in your arms and lap and cry my eyes out with snot all over my face as childhood memories flooded me. Thank you for when the Kleenex box was empty at the end you would remind me to invite Jesus into the pain to heal me. Thank you for speaking over my life to write this experience down on paper so others could experience the same kind of healing I received. You mean the world to me, and it is a relationship that would be hard to explain to anybody but us.

My favorite friend Michelle Lyons, who loves to secretly pray and encourage people. You have stuck by my side through it all. When I wanted to give up you always encouraged me to keep going as you proofread my chapters. I love you and I can't wait to travel the world with you.

To Kristen Stieffel. When we first met at a writing conference in 2015, you kind of intimidated me as a really smart person. But after several editors not being the right fit, I then reached out to you, and we immediately clicked. You are the best writing mentor and editor a friend could ask for. Thank you for encouraging me and being patient enough to teach me about this new writing world.

One last note from me, if you are reading this book and you know me personally or maybe you were a part of my story. This book was never written to hurt or shame anyone. This is my story written to help others and let them know there is a way out. Just remember that we all have different perspectives, and it's okay. May God speak to your heart in these next few pages.

With grace and love,

Paula Jauch

author's note

This book illustrates my life's journey and struggles from my perspective. Due to all the trauma, I have lost a lot of childhood memories. To some my story might be a bit overwhelming, but it is my story and my experience, and I can no longer hide behind shame and secrets. Today I live my life as a child of God and woman in recovery.

Regardless of why you picked up this book, I want to encourage you that—whether you have had experience with addiction or abuse, whether it was a personal addiction, being raised in addiction, or loving someone who struggles with addiction—there is hope for healing, if you are willing to do the work and trust God with all your heart and soul.

If my story helps just one person heal from trauma and addiction, then I have achieved my goal.

Paula Jauch
paula@paulajauch.com

CHAPTER 1

what's wrong with me?

Have you ever felt like you were different from everyone else? I have—deeply to the core of my being I never felt like anybody else. Perhaps you've felt that way, too—feelings of insecurity, fear, and self-doubt that you are constantly doing it all wrong.

The nagging voices in my head were loud. I could no longer fight the torment I was feeling. At age 21, I was renting a house in Las Vegas with the help of a government program. My three children were between the ages of 6 months and 6 years old. This was a time that they needed their mommy but the feeling to relieve myself of the pain was greater than their needs at the time. You may not understand this, but this is a true feeling that comes with suicidal thoughts.

I remember walking into my bedroom that day, opening the door of my closet, and shutting myself in. I sat on the floor processing how I could stop the dark feelings. I was a cutter, so I thought, *maybe if I cut a little deeper that would stop the pain.*

As I sat there on the floor contemplating suicide, out of nowhere my thoughts shifted, and I started to see all the people over the years who told me that God loves me and has a plan for my life. I started to wrestle with these thoughts, and I began to weep. My 6-year-old opened the door and looked at me. He said, "I hate you, Mommy. All you do is cry!" He slammed the door and walked away. Then I heard the voice of an old coworker, *Jesus loves you, and He wants to heal your heart.* When she spoke these words to me, I really didn't care what she had to say. It was confusing for me to understand, and she was way too happy for me to even try to receive what she was saying.

But at that moment in the closet, I felt a nudge not to give up. Then in the midst of my hopelessness I opened my mouth and cried out to God, "If you are real, I *need* to know you now!" It was a cry for help.

Next thing you know, something felt different in the atmosphere. I felt different. As I lay there on the closet floor, it felt as if a peace had penetrated my heart. That peace was something that I had never experienced before, and I wanted to tell someone who would understand what was going on. Then I thought of my neighbor, the annoying guy who kept putting Jesus pamphlets on my car before I would go to work. I placed my babies on the couch and looked at each one in the face. I told them mommy would be right back and with confidence in my voice I said, "Your mommy is never going to be the same." I just knew that something in my heart had changed. I ran across the street to my neighbor's house and told him what happened. With joy on his face, he came over to my house and laid his hand on my shoulder and started to pray with me. The next Sunday he invited me to church.

The Stories I Made Up

The battle I faced for many years made me feel different from other people and gave me a sense that I didn't belong. When I went into public places, I assumed people could see all the issues I was trying to hide. Such fear gripped me that I imagined that everyone was talking about me. (I guess I thought I was so important that everybody was focused on me all the time.) But, it was my self-consciousness stirring up inside. I made up stories about what other people were thinking and saying about me, and those stories became my go-to narrative.

When I met people for the first time, I had already predetermined that they weren't going to like me and I treated them as such. I avoided eye contact and engaging in conversation with them. I behaved this way as early as I can remember, starting around age five.

My father was incarcerated for ten years, and my mother was absent because of a gambling addiction. It seemed normal, and I wasn't aware that my needs weren't being met. It was just the way things were. Children don't know what is normal and what's not. I see it every day—adults who are still broken from their childhood and still acting and behaving like wounded children.

I believed that something was wrong with me: I didn't understand that someone had wronged me, causing trauma.

The Voices in My Head

My self-hate became stronger in my teen years, and I tried many ways to escape the confusion and pain. After being placed in special education classes in middle school, my anger started to manifest. I felt such shame when I would have to go to the special classes because all my friends would know. After school, I would go home to an empty house when my dad was in prison and my mom was gone to the casino or work. I would sit in my room alone with some type of sharp object; it was usually the metal from my pencil after I took off the eraser. As I sat in my room with nowhere to turn with my feelings, I would cut my legs and wrist by rubbing the metal part of the pencil in a back-and-forth motion.

When I looked in the mirror, I couldn't see the real me. I couldn't see the person God created me to be. It was like looking into a damaged mirror—a warped image. All I could see was someone who was stupid, fat, ugly, and funny looking.

The voices in my head got louder and more insistent: *There is something terribly wrong with you. You need to fix yourself.*

The voices in my head were louder than reality and activated a war inside me but I could not explain it to anybody because I didn't know what was happening. When this war took place, I would stand in front of the bathroom mirror. This bathroom was in the process of being remodeled for years. The shower was broken, and it became a storage for all the material to fix the bathroom one day. These were the types of conditions we lived in. Standing in front of the mirror I asked myself the question, *why are you even here?* Nobody likes you. Then using my fist, I punched my face until I had bumps on my forehead or bruising on my cheeks.

As an adult, "fixing" myself and especially my body image became my obsession. Later in my mid-thirties, a trauma therapist diagnosed me with Dysmorphia. Someone with Dysmorphia looks in the mirror and sees some abnormality or deformity in the shape or size of specific body parts. That description fit me well. My obsession with wanting to change myself became one of my addictions. I spent a lot of time and money on weight-loss products such as pills, books, diet plans, and much more. I was stuck in a cycle of binge eating and purging. It did a lot of damage to my body to the point that I needed surgery. What I later learned after working through my healing process was that my obsession to want to look like someone else was really a way of wanting to escape my present situation. When my trauma would get triggered by a person, place, or thing, then these behaviors became more intense in my life.

I felt crippled on the inside and desperately wanted to be free from the torment I was suffering. I wanted to like myself. I wanted to be liked by other people and I wanted to feel confident in my skin, but my inner struggle of hating myself blocked me from this change that I so longed for.

Due to my struggle when other people tried to have a conversation with me, I could not focus on what they were saying. I was always gripped with shame and secrets, so I couldn't hear a word they were saying. I didn't know it then, but trauma was driving my fear of rejection and the voices in my head.

Snap Out of It?

I often wished I could snap out of how I was feeling, but I couldn't. If you know someone who is in the depths of trauma like I was, please don't say, "snap out of it" or "just get over it already." Or worse—"just pray more." Now I realize that telling myself to snap out of trauma was like telling someone else to "snap out of a coma." A disconnect was going on inside me. This behavior made it hard for me to function as an adult woman.

Operating in a work environment was difficult. I didn't know how to handle constructive criticism or feedback. If my boss or coworkers tried to talk to me about anything, I walked away feeling like a child who just got shamed, even if their voices were calm and professional. I used to write down things they said so I wouldn't forget.

I remember my first job interview after graduating from high school. At this young age, I already had two children with my abusive boyfriend who had introduced me to the gang life in Las Vegas where we lived. Because I was born into a family of addiction and neglect, I longed to belong, and the gang seemed to provide the acceptance I craved. School had been a struggle; I was placed in special education classes and various behavioral programs until I was kicked out and sent to an alternative education program.

I was thrilled to get this job interview for clerical work. It made me feel valued and important. Excited and nervous, I sat restless in my seat as the three women interviewing me glanced at my application.

One of the women gave me a hesitant look. "We are very concerned after looking at your job application. There was a lot of misspelling on it. Do you have trouble in this area?"

I felt my face flush as I sat there and recalled all the years I struggled in school to learn like everybody else. I don't remember my response, but I imagine the words stuck in my throat. I knew I had struggled in school but I didn't know that I had trouble with spelling or pronouncing words properly. I walked out of that interview thinking, *there must be something wrong with me. Why can't I do this basic skill?*

This conscious thought of lack and embarrassment was nothing compared to the damage done at the subconscious level. At this point, you are probably wondering how I could not know I had trouble with reading. I will explain more of that to you, but first allow me to define what subconscious means.

Subconscious: a part of your mind or existing thought that you are not fully aware of, but it influences your actions and feelings. In the case of the job interview, I was embarrassed and upset in the moment, but quickly pushed all the unpleasant feelings down into my subconscious. In that hidden place, the humiliation built up tremendous power over me. *You are stupid, you can't spell … What's wrong with you?* My bottled-up belief controlled my actions and behaviors and filled me with shame.

I didn't realize I was broken. I was living life the best I could. I took full responsibility as if *I* had caused my problems, as if I had wounded myself. As if my actions and choices as a child had led to that awful moment at the job interview.

Being unsure of myself caused me to accept a lot of unacceptable behaviors in relationships because I didn't know how to protect myself or discern healthy boundaries. Many people took advantage of my obvious weaknesses. I was deeply vulnerable and didn't even realize it. My inner struggle held me back from having healthy relationships, because in my traumatized state, I was not going to attract healthy people into my life.

These thoughts—that there-is-something-wrong-but-I'm-not-sure-what-it-is feeling—holds us captive and stops us from accomplishing what we dream. I longed to have a normal life, even though I didn't know what *normal* was at the time. I still wanted normalcy. I often daydreamed about healthy relationships, job promotions, and enjoying simple things like being a good mom. Success seemed out of reach for someone like me.

I know I'm not the only one who has felt this way. When I speak at schools, churches, or women's groups about my story, people tell me they can relate. You and I are not alone in the struggle.

If you're like me, you won't recognize this broken internal dialogue until you have spent several years in unhealthy relationships, stuck in a cycle of self-destructive behaviors, bound to addiction, or living a life of severe limits because of this battle.

Isn't this idea crazy? But common—and true. What's even more heartbreaking is to think about those folks who have taken their dreams to the grave with them because they were not able to get free from what held them back.

Let's not be characterized by our past.

My friend, it all starts in the mind. Somewhere something happened to us to cause us to believe, *there is something wrong with me.* Yes, I am calling it a "belief system" because belief is all it really is. But, oh! The life-controlling, life-diminishing power these ideas have over you and me until we learn how to uproot and replace lies with truth.

Today, my trauma no longer controls my life and choices. Please don't get me wrong, there are certain people, places, and things that trigger me, but I remind myself that I am safe today. I never thought I would be in a healthy marriage, pursuing my God-given dreams, and thriving in my work. But getting to this point took hard work. I certainly didn't "snap out of it," and neither will you. One of the first steps for me was going back to the beginning, to when these negative seeds were planted in my life.

Back to my earliest memory of neglect. Remembering how my father would come in and out of our home from his drunken binges. Recalling how I was left anywhere with anyone, because my mom was busy chasing him around and trying to fix him.

Thinking of the times my mother would stay away from our home for nights due to her gambling addiction and how I had to try to find ways to feed my little brother and myself.

Considering the long days I struggled to raise my first child at the age of fifteen when trying to survive myself.

You might be thinking that it is too painful to go back and try to pinpoint what is causing *your* pain. You might even be saying, "I don't need to look at my past," or "my childhood wasn't that bad." I hear this kind of logic often. Then I watch people stay stuck in the same old patterns that are making them miserable.

The truth is, we can't heal from what we are not willing to feel. Let me repeat this major principle because I want you to soak it in. *We can't heal from what we are not willing to feel.*

I know firsthand how hard it is to get past all of this. I truly understand how it feels to stay stuck and bury my emotions. And I know the work that needs to be done. If I had never taken the time to do the work, I wouldn't be able to write this book and share my story of healing with you.

Please be open-minded as you read through these pages. I don't know all the answers—But God has healed my broken heart, and His healing has helped me in numerous areas of my life, including in the area of relationships.

The Relationship that Almost Killed Me

By the time I met my first boyfriend, I felt damaged. But when he came into my life with his baggage and past behaviors, he ignited my trauma and opened my wounds.

Our relationship started out innocently enough. I was in the seventh grade and met a boy who had a crush on me. As I was sitting in class, he passed a note to me. He traced his hand on some lined paper and wrote the words *Hi, you're pretty*. He then folded it up and passed it through the row of students to me.

After I received the note, he continued to befriend me. We started to hang out together a lot at school. He began to walk me home every day after school.

As we started spending a lot of time together, we discovered we had a lot in common. His father was deceased from a drinking and driving car accident, and my father was in prison. Both of our mothers were gone a lot because of work and trying to manage a single-parent household.

I learned pretty quickly he was very street smart. He was able to teach me a lot of skills—like smoking marijuana, drinking, and fighting—that would soon become my new ways of coping. He filled the big void in my life left by my absent parents. It felt good to finally have someone give me attention and want to spend time with me. It was probably not the best attention, but at least it gave me some sense of worth.

He made me feel good about myself. Even the very basic words like "you are pretty" fed my attention-starved soul.

After spending many days and nights with him, I discovered that he belonged to a large Hispanic gang, which introduced me to a whole new world I was not familiar with. I was just a little white girl who had lived on a farm until my parents moved our family to Las Vegas when I was eight.

After a short time of hanging out with him, I was adopted into the gang family. It was a family that was loyal and would do anything for each other, even give their lives.

To become a member of this gang, you had to be initiated in. A few male gang members jumped me in by taking me out into a Las Vegas desert and began kicking and punching me. I was already good at numbing pain. And this physical pain was overshadowed by the sense of belonging.

My reasoning may sound twisted unless you understand my pain and trauma, but I was desperate for attention and to have someone in my life. I felt like I was finally part of something. It felt like I finally had people in my life who cared.

It was easy to adapt to gang life. You didn't need to be rich; you didn't need to be educated; and you didn't need attentive parents. In fact, attentive parents were a huge negative. The less your parents cared, the better, as far as the gang was concerned. Recruits like me just needed to be teachable and become street smart.

I quickly felt comfortable in this environment and with my new boyfriend it felt like the perfect match for me. I had a relationship with this boy for the next fourteen years. From age thirteen until I was twenty-seven. We grew up together. I was raised with violence in my home, so every time my boyfriend hit me, it felt normal. His abuse and aggression fueled my own aggression, and I started getting kicked out of school for fighting.

Every time he called me a demeaning name, it felt natural. Every time he cheated on me, it felt like business as usual. However, the cheating triggered the old familiar neglect and rejection. The cheating reinforced the story I told myself. *See, there is something wrong with me. Otherwise he would have been faithful.* That old rejection wound was opened again and again, and my trauma grew. Eventually, I turned to more drugs and alcohol to cope.

By the time I was twenty-one years old, I had three small children with him. I was willing to do anything to keep him from leaving.

The Messages We Receive

No wonder I was wounded and filled with fear and self-hate. I did not experience a loving, safe environment, and I had experienced so much abuse. Can you see the messages I was receiving? *You are not lovable. There must be something wrong with you. Everybody leaves you.* My mother was always gone, my father was in prison, and I had children with someone who was constantly cheating on me. The messages I got from these people confirmed my self-hate. *I am not good enough.*

Living this way is trauma. Now, you may have heard the word trauma tossed around, but do you know what it means? SAMHSA (Substance Abuse and Mental Health Services Agency) describes individual trauma as resulting from "an event, series of events, or set of circumstances that is experienced by an individual as physically or emotionally harmful or life threatening and that has lasting adverse effects on the individual's functioning and mental, physical, social, emotional, or spiritual well-being."

According to SAMHSA, research has shown that traumatic experiences are associated with both behavioral health and chronic physical health conditions, especially those traumatic events that occur during childhood. Substance use (such as smoking, excessive alcohol use, and taking drugs), mental health conditions (such as depression, anxiety, or PTSD), and other risky behaviors (such as self-injury and risky sexual encounters) have been linked with traumatic experiences. Because these behavioral health concerns can present challenges in relationships, careers, and other aspects of life, it is important to understand the nature and impact of trauma, and to explore healing.

No one should have to go through trauma, but too many of us do. In the United States, 61 percent of men and 51 percent of women report exposure to at least one lifetime traumatic event.

You may be reading my story with compassion right now. *Poor girl*, you may be thinking. *She didn't stand a chance with those parents and that upbringing. Of course, she would believe there was something wrong with her, but her problems were caused by others.*

I challenge you to also have compassion for others—and for yourself. You may not have experienced nearly the same level of trauma as me, but any kind of trauma makes you feel as if something is wrong with you.

Now remember that with every negative life experience you encounter, you pick up a negative belief and store it in your subconscious brain.

At this point in your life, you have probably had some difficult experiences. Maybe someone spoke something about you or to you that was hurtful, or someone who should have loved you or protected you instead physically or sexually abused you. These occurrences planted the negative beliefs into your mind that there must be something wrong with you. We start operating out of fear and entrenched feelings of not being good enough.

Then we start to perform by trying to work harder, look better, so we can be accepted. At least this was my case.

As time passes, we don't like the pressure that we are feeling on the inside, so we try to find some way of escape. Coming to this decision, we decide to take control. We may try to control other people out of fear of not wanting to be hurt or neglected again. We might try to control our pain through some sort of addiction or self-destructive behaviors. We spend years of our lives stuck, going around and around the same mountain, but none of our attempts touch the core issue. What started the pain in the first place? What messages did you and I receive to spark the terrible feelings of unworthiness?

Nobody likes these feelings. We never asked for trauma, and we aren't born with it. Damaged emotions are curable. You can be healed and restored to your true identity, but first you must take the time to see when, where, and how these feelings started.

My goal is to make sure that what I am trying to say sinks deep into your heart. There is hope for your situation, no matter where you are in life. And if you fall or you have failed in the past, get up and try again.

I love what this verse in the Bible states, "The godly may trip seven times, but they will get up again. But one disaster is enough to overthrow the wicked" (Proverbs 24:16 NLT).

I don't care what age you are when you pick up this book. I don't care if you are sitting in a jail cell or a mansion. If you are still breathing, God is not finished with you.

You may feel like you are behind on your game but remember if you are reading this, you are still alive and there is still time for God to do His amazing work in your life. I want to help you to break free from this pattern so you can start to live a life of freedom filled with joy.

The first step is realizing there is nothing inherently wrong with you or me. However, it was the wrong done *to* us that caused our trauma and our battles. Only when we have separated fact from fiction, can we finally break free from the family dysfunction, neglect, and abuse we once thought was okay.

reflection

Imagine Jesus is sitting in the room with you. Even if you were like me in the beginning, and you are not sure if God exists, repeat this prayer by faith. One thing I do know for sure is what the verse below states—before we start our day, we need to be filled with His truth, knowing that He loves us no matter the past choices we have made or what has happened to us. He knows our pain, and He knows the pain we have endured. I promise you, He will never let you down. Even when your situation doesn't make sense, He is still there.

1. After reading parts of my story and my everyday struggles, can you relate to it in any way? Do you struggle with any of the same thoughts or beliefs that plagued me?

2. What about escaping? Are there any areas of your life that you regret and are you trying to escape through some form of addiction or coping mechanism? Take some time right now to write out your answers. Be specific and honest with yourself.

3. As you were reading some of the events in my life that caused overwhelming emotions, negative thoughts, or even addictive behavior, did any memories of your life flash through your mind? I want you to write those memories. Write how they made you feel. Were you angry, scared, or sad? Did you feel violated, unloved, or unprotected?

prayer

Dear God,

I am tired of doing it my way. My way is no longer working, and it's not making my pain go away. I feel so tired and exhausted, and I am ready for peace and joy in my life. Please give me the willingness to do whatever it takes to heal and become a whole person. Right now, I am trusting you to heal all of me, my soul, and all my past wounds. I am asking you to forgive me for my sins. Please come live in my heart and take over my life. I am laying down my way and my will. I am asking you by faith to bring the people, places, and resources I need in order to recover and become the person you created me to be. Amen.

scripture

"Let me hear of your unfailing love each morning, for I am trusting you. Show me where to walk, for I give myself to you"
(Psalm 143:8 NLT).

CHAPTER 2

finding my normal

Parents who struggle with an addiction are often absent from the home and from their child and are often unaware of the effect on their children. They typically downplay their behavior by saying children are resilient and will get over it. This excuse gives the parent temporary relief from their guilt and shame while the child is still suffering. Many children of parents with alcoholism and drug addiction know it's difficult to rebound from the trauma of such a childhood.

I can feel the fan blowing on my face like it was yesterday and still hear my sweet, innocent, little-girl voice reciting the prayer, "Now I lay me down to sleep, I pray the Lord my soul to keep. If I should die before I awake, I pray the Lord my soul to take." I repeated this prayer often as a little girl, and to be quite honest, I am not even sure where I learned it. Maybe it was something I picked up from my short time of attending a Catholic school in the first grade.

Most nights, my brothers and I slept on the floor. Every house usually had more children than beds or bedrooms. We liked to make a bed on the floor, and we called it the pallet. Each of us would lay a blanket on the floor and put the fan right in front of our face. It was usually a fight every night over who would get the middle spot where we could feel the fan blowing the most. When our parents moved my sister, my four brothers, and me from our small town in Indiana to Las Vegas in the desert, the fan became a big deal in our house, since the weather often reached as high as 116 degrees.

The older I get, I'm amazed how life tends to work. Some memories are remembered like it happened yesterday, and some memories my mind chooses to forget—I believe in order to protect me. Sometimes my life can be a bit of a blur, but the older I get and the longer I walk through my healing journey of acceptance, I believe God allows some memories to surface because I need to remember so I can heal.

Missed Childhood

I feel I missed much of my childhood because there are so many memories that I am unable to recall. Especially when I see pictures of myself as a little girl, I don't remember being present. I believe forgetting is a shelter from some of the distress my pure little soul was exposed to. One of those precious gifts was the little prayer I recited often to get me through nights of fear.

Some nights I would be awakened by screaming or breaking glass. Too often, one of my older siblings would stand in the way and take the blows to keep my father from hurting my mother or a younger child during one of my father's drunken rages. The rest of us comforted each other through the sounds of screams of terror and pain.

When I was a newborn, my sister had to take care of me a lot, and she was only nine years old. I couldn't imagine having that type of responsibility at her age. She said there were nights when I would not stop crying, and she didn't know what to do with me. *What nine-year-old would?* Back then, most bottles were made out of glass. She said she chucked my bottle across the room, shattering it everywhere. Then she fell on her knees and started crying with me.

Now imagine that picture: a scared little nine-year-old girl trying to take care of a screaming newborn. At that age, my sister should have been in her room playing with her dolls or playing hide-n-seek outside with her friends, not being left alone to babysit all of her younger siblings.

Do childhood experiences affect our lives as adults? I know they do. Our upbringing can have a negative or a positive effect on our lives.

At this point in your life, the negative effects of your childhood are probably why you chose to read this book—to try to make sense of the patterns you keep repeating? As we get older and mature, our belief system is being shaped by our childhood experiences. What we believe about ourselves and the way we see ourselves stems from what we were taught and what we heard and saw as children.

I won't repeat some of the names my father called me growing up, nor am I willing to give you a long list of all I feel he has done wrong. That's not my goal. But let me be clear—no child should have witnessed or experienced what I saw as a child. Unfortunately, abuse happens all the time to many children. Your story could be far worse than mine.

A Choice to Heal

What's important is that we can heal from our negative childhood experiences if we get the proper help. It's a choice to heal. I want to encourage you to take the steps to do so. That way you can be free to have a life that God intended you to live.

I could never quite figure out why I was always drawn to people who mistreated me. After I was an adult and had some time in a recovery program, I learned we are usually drawn to relationships that remind us of our childhood. My first boyfriend was abusive and controlling just like my father—and he struggled with addictions, too. I stayed in an unhealthy relationship with him for fourteen years because I couldn't escape the patterns and history of my life.

It was all I knew since the day I was born: chaos and dysfunction and abuse.

I was used to it.

As I sat in the cold room of an emergency room at the hospital waiting for a doctor to come in my body was shivering, and I was not sure if it was from the pain or from being cold. Emotions and fear were running through me as I was trying to figure out what I should tell the doctor. Do I tell him it's a car accident or that my boyfriend beat me up? I was having trouble opening my mouth from being punched in the jaw, and it was hard to breathe from being kicked so many times in the ribs.

I'm embarrassed to say this, but it took many of these kinds of scenarios to finally get to my point of desperation.

My body was becoming tired and worn out. I didn't have the fight in me to keep up with all the hiding and secrets from my children, my family, friends, and trying to keep a job. The exhaustion was taking over. My body was crying surrender. When the father of my three children would stay out drinking all night, I noticed that I actually started to enjoy it instead of staying up all night crying with fear and anxiety.

When I finally realized that this relationship was seriously wrong, I often wondered, *Do all men act this way? Are they all abusers and beaters? This was a belief system of mine that I had for a very long time because of what I experienced with my earthly father and my first long-term boyfriend. It was not an easy one to break free.*

At this point, I was tired of my life and the situation I was living in. My misery drove me to start asking questions. *Is this normal?* I know, this a simple question, and it seems there is probably no right or wrong answer, but I needed to know. *Was everything that I'd been through in my life normal?* If it was, then why did I feel unhappy all the time, to the point where I felt like I wanted to take my own life? Deep inside, I knew there had to be a different way of living than how I was raised. There has to be more to life than struggling all the time in every area. I was tired of living a life that felt like a constant battle.

When I started going to a Christian church for the first time, and I was sitting in a Bible study and the pastor's wife was teaching on something I can't even remember, I recall blurting out really loud can you really live a life of peace and happiness? Don't worry I was just a baby Christian at the time desperate for change. I remember her looking at me really confused probably thinking where did that come from?

My childhood home was filled with addiction, screaming, fighting, infidelity, and poverty. My father would be gone for months at a time— sometimes on drinking binges or away in a mental hospital. During my teen years, he was sent to prison.

I once asked a trusted friend, "Is it normal to fear your father and his behaviors, yet miss him so much that it hurts?" I needed someone to validate how I was feeling. I was confused to have these types of feelings toward someone who you are supposed to love and respect. I think it was even harder on me since my mother tolerated his behavior, which was even more confusing to me. But my friend helped me understand that everyone, especially a child, longs to be loved by a father—but she made it very clear to point out that my earthly father's behaviors and how he treated me was inappropriate and abuse. It's not okay to call your young child names that they should never hear or offer them to do drugs with you.

In my mid-twenties something started to shift in my life. I constantly felt this uneasiness inside me that wasn't at peace with my surroundings. I was no longer comfortable in the places where I once was okay. I remember at age 21 just after having my third baby, and I went to my dad's house for a family event. When I walked in the garage, everybody was drinking, and then I saw lines of cocaine on the table. At that moment, I could have snorted a line just like I would have in the past. *I thought it would help me lose all my baby weight and have the energy to clean my home.* But that day, I thought, *I am going to somehow get my children and me out of here as fast as I can.* I had to put time limits on people and on the places where I used to hang around and start seeking comfort in new places like my new church family, women's Bible studies, and my recovery program.

A Gentle Voice

At this point in my life, I kept hearing a gentle voice guiding me, telling me *all this drinking and drug use and violence is not normal,* and *you no longer have to be around it.*

I learned to listen to this voice through the new Christian music I was listening to, a sermon at church, a new healthy friend, or my time alone journaling and dreaming about a different life. During this season is when my true self was desiring to rise up and come forth, even though it felt scary to think the opposite of all I ever knew. I was losing my desire to party with my friends or to attend family functions that had alcohol or fighting. At first I wondered if something was wrong with me. Was I being judgmental, or was I desperate for peace.

When I look back now, I can clearly see God was at work. I believe He knew I was getting to the bottom and wanting to give up. I am going to let you in on a little secret that I have never shared before. When I was a newly saved Christian, I was still in this abusive relationship, still trying to fix the father of my children, and make it work. But when I sat in church I noticed this really cute worship leader who was not married, and I used to fantasize what would my life look like if I was married to someone like that? Looking back now, I understand this is not a bad thing to dream about. The father of my children was selling drugs for an income, and he was involved with the gang life. Looking back now I feel God was showing me a whole new way of living. An important key that I have learned in life is that you become who you associate with, and this is why I knew it was time to leave.

Children, who have experienced trauma in their lives from any kind of physical, emotional, or sexual abuse or who have grown up in addiction are usually confused about what they have seen or what has happened to them. Something doesn't seem right, yet they are unsure of what is right.

Do these children dare ask questions or speak up? Most children who have been affected by addiction or abuse are afraid to ask questions. They may feel guilty. And they don't want to disappoint anyone or be abused again. The fear and guilt are especially real in relation to those who are authority figures in their lives. Sometimes parents even encourage their children not to talk, trust, or feel.

Children of abuse live with or bury their memories to protect themselves from the trauma they have experienced. But these memories can cause a lot of problems when buried alive, especially when they start to come back and flash through our minds.

We often start to question ourselves by asking if we are making up the memories, or we second-guess ourselves because the memories are not clear. As we start to remember, we often only remember bits and pieces—usually what we can handle at the moment. We start to downplay it and tell ourselves it wasn't that bad, so we can still keep it a secret.

Keeping what we have witnessed as children a secret can make us sick. It usually leaves us with symptoms of anxiety, fear, depression, insomnia, and self-hate. According to Adverse Childhood Experiences and Trauma Informed Care for Educators, most children have experienced some type of trauma before the age four, and these traumatic experiences play a huge role in who they become. Trauma affects our behaviors and our feelings and causes many adults to live with unnecessary turmoil.

I'm sure you've heard the saying, "We become as sick as our secrets." I wish parents knew the damage they cause when their children don't grow up feeling safe, nurtured, loved, provided for, and protected. But too often, the parents are also wounded individuals.

Understanding the impact of a parent was a huge eye-opener for me when I was raising my children, and I can see how my children suffered because I lacked skills in so many areas—due to my upbringing. I was a wounded soul wounding my children. Not on purpose. I never received affection from my parents, so it was difficult for me to hug and kiss my children.

When my kids hugged me, I felt awkward. I attempted to breastfeed one of my children, but due to my sexual abuse, I felt violated having my infant suck from my breast. Just thinking of it today gives me chills. I know this is not the way God created us, but triggers from my past trauma prevented me from being the parent I wanted to be.

With all the knowledge I have today—my life experience—I thank God for His love and mercies. I've learned so much through my healing and recovery journey. He's taught me how to break many strongholds I thought I had to live with, and I started by forgiving myself.

Today I am aware of my character defects. I can learn from them and grow. Through my new learned behaviors, I can make amends to my children for what I was unable to give them.

Believe me, becoming a better parent did not happen overnight. My children and I are still healing, and I'm still making mistakes and learning as I go. But I am quicker to admit when I'm wrong and listen to others today. When I was filled with so much pain, I was self-centered, which made it hard to attend to my children's needs. In the beginning of learning my new behaviors, there were many days I had to *fake it* until those behaviors became my new normal.

I was already a young mommy to three children by the time I was twenty-one years old. I remember turning twenty-one thinking now I can party all the time, and I don't have to stand in front of the liquor store to ask people to buy me alcohol. I was getting tired of using the fake ID I'd had since I was fifteen—plus it didn't work all the time.

But something happened to me after I had that encounter with Jesus in my closet. When my friends came over to my house to party and get drunk and high, I started to feel uncomfortable in that environment, although it had been my "normal" for so long. I remember trying to make excuses to get them to leave my house. Then I started using my kids as an excuse for why I couldn't go out to the nightclubs or parties anymore.

One night when I was about twenty-one I had a kind of vision where

I saw myself standing in a puddle of water filled with mud. The mud was gummy and smelly, and I didn't like how it felt. I felt uncomfortable and stuck. I watched people as they walked past me. Some of them looked happy, and they didn't have any mud on them. Part of me asked questions, *Should I be standing in this mud? Is this normal?*

I wanted to get out of the mud, but I didn't know how and I was afraid getting out was impossible. Slowly I started to climb out of the mud, and it felt weird at first. I felt guilty because my friends and family were still in the mud. I climbed out of the mud hole. A small voice whispered, *I have planned much more for your life than this.*

I started to follow the nudge that kept reassuring me there was more to life than mud. With every step I took out of the mud, tools were being placed in my hands to help me. The key was I had to search for those tools with my hands open, and I had to be willing to leave the old to find the new. I started meeting new people who were on the same path as me and some who had gone before me and could pull me in the way I needed to keep going. They shared hope for my situation and helped me believe that I could heal from my childhood, as long as I was willing to do the work.

I learned about a recovery program and started to attend the weekly meetings immediately. I discovered I wasn't alone. Other people sitting around the table wanted to get out of the mud, too. Each person wanted a new way of life and each one was finding it through their relationship with God and fellow travelers in the recovery program.

My new friends in the recovery program reassured me that there is another way of living that doesn't consist of the mud (addiction, abuse, alcohol, and dysfunction.) I longed for their words to be true, so I kept coming back.

Not too long after being grounded in my new recovery program, I found a local church, which my children and I started to attend. At this church, I received the same message. You don't have to stay in the mud. God has a better plan for your life. I became hungry for what these people were saying.

When I wasn't at church or my recovery program, I still had to deal with those friends and family who were still standing in the mud. I loved these people deeply. Leaving the mud and joining a recovery program and a church was not easy because they would say, "Who do you think you are? You belong here." They said I was not the same person anymore, and they made me second-guess the new path I was on. So, more times than I would like to admit, I jumped back into the mud with them. But each time, I felt hopeless and doomed. So I dragged myself back out of the mud and ran the opposite direction to the people who told me I didn't have to go back there.

You and I don't have to stay where we no longer feel comfortable even though some people—people we love—are not going to like it when we start to change. You can take control of your life if you are unhappy and long for a different way of living. Take some time to reevaluate your life or current circumstances.

What is normal? You can discover your normal. Begin by making a list of life situations or conditions you want to change. Then start searching for the tools that can get you to that new normal. For example, if you are struggling with an addiction, look for a local recovery program. If you've experienced sexual abuse, look for a good therapist who specializes in this area. Connect with those who are capable of walking you through your trauma. I suggest you get recommendations from trustworthy sources or a recommendation from a good friend.

You must be ready for a change and determined to go to any measure to get help. I often meet people who say they are ready for a change but are not willing to leave the mud or do whatever it takes to find help. The main reason is because people don't want to deal with their pain.

Don't give up if you don't feel comfortable with the first therapist you see, find another. If I had quit, I wouldn't be where I am today.

Recovery isn't easy because you must break away from loved ones and old habits that helped you survive in the past. But if you want to get better, you have to be willing to let go so there is room for new possibilities.

It will be scary at first. Please remember becoming whole is a process, and it's not going to happen overnight. It may take years to completely break away from all the pain you have experienced. I had to learn to work on my behaviors slowly. Even though my deepest desire was to change, my self-destructive behaviors seemed to keep popping up their ugly heads. But my new and trusted friends reminded me I was growing and encouraged me to keep my eyes on how far I have come.

As we walk through our healing journeys, it is important for us to remember we didn't ask to be born into dysfunctional families. And we didn't have any say over the abuses and injustices we experienced. But the more we touch and embrace our stories, the sooner we can heal.

Acceptance plays a huge role in the healing process. What a tricky word—acceptance. We aren't required or encouraged to agree with or like what happened to us, but we need to accept, admit, and acknowledge our story.

For a long time, I was ashamed of my story. I thought my bad experiences must somehow be my fault. But when I was able to recognize my story for what it was and walk through all the emotions that came with it, I started to get better. I needed to grieve the losses, be angry at what happened to me, then forgive those who hurt me. As I followed these steps—sometimes two steps forward and one step backward—my miracle started to happen. I started to find peace and joy.

Good Questions

I would like to share part of a Bible story that has helped me a lot. Even if you don't read the Bible, observe how the guy in the story handled his hardships. His story is found in the Old Testament book in the Bible, Job. If you have a Bible, I encourage you to read it. If you've read the story before, I encourage you to read it again. The reason I want to use Job's story is because when Job experienced the worst possible life situations, he asked God hard questions, and he expressed deep emotions.

Job understood what it was like to suffer. In the midst of his suffering he said, "How frail is humanity! How short is life, how full of trouble! We blossom like a flower and then wither. Like a passing shadow, we quickly disappear. Must you keep an eye on such a frail creature and demand an accounting from me? Who can bring purity out of an impure person? No one!" (Job 14:1–4 NLT).

These were good questions. How frail is humanity? How short is life, how full of trouble?

Life is full of trouble, my friend; life brings a lot of heartache. And yes, we are like a passing shadow that will soon disappear. That is why each of us needs to make the most out of our life. This life doesn't always make sense, and people who are supposed to love us will neglect us and hurt us.

When you read Job's story, you see how persistent his hard questions were. I believe he asked the hard questions because he knew God's character to be good, faithful, and fair—even when life wasn't easy. As you read Job's story, you will see his honest emotions and questions to God. Yet he never stopped seeking God.

I don't believe we can ever ask God a wrong question. To be honest, there will be times when you ask Him hard questions and feel like you aren't getting any answers. These moments are when your faith needs to kick into gear—trusting that He is moving on our behalf. There is another scripture in the Bible that I hold close to my heart, "Trust in the Lord with all your heart; do not depend on your own understanding. Seek his will in all you do, and he will show you which path to take" (Proverbs 3: 5–7 NLT).

If you feel you need further support or comfort, begin with prayer, and then call a friend from church or a friend in recovery. Just make sure it's someone who understands the road you are traveling.

Remember, only those who are willing to work through the pain and unfairness of life and still seek God will find the peace they are searching for. Those who seek Him will find Him. It's time to rest in the loving arms of the one who created you. This is where you will find the answers you've been searching for, not the things this world has to offer you.

reflection

We will begin to heal by acknowledging the damage that was done to us in our childhood. With the help of God and trusted friends, we gain the courage to face painful memories.

1. At this present time in your life, how would you define *normal*? Is your perception distorted? Are you okay with your life today? If you are having a hard time answering these questions, that's okay. Move to the next question. Sometimes we need to take time to heal to discover our new normal.
2. What are some hard questions you want to ask God? When asking

your questions, remember God already knows what you've been through and how you feel. Nothing is going to be a surprise to Him. Take some time to sit still as you write these questions out. What is that still small voice inside of you saying?

3. What are some emotions that you are feeling? Can you label them? If not, do you think it's time to find a therapist or a recovery program to help you sort through these emotions? Sometimes when we are overloaded with emotions, it can feel like our head is full of spaghetti noodles.

prayer

Dear God,
I am ready to trust you with all my feelings and emotions. Even though I don't know what that kind of trust looks like, I am still going to trust you. I am asking you to bring me the right resources and support in my life that will help to heal and to start to understand what is normal. I am asking you to give me a boldness to start asking hard questions so I can face the truth of what was and learn to start to accept what has happened to me. Today I am choosing to trust you with all my heart by faith. I'm ready for my life to be restored to how you meant it to be. I am releasing all my fears and bottled up emotions to you today. Amen.

scripture

"Trust in the Lord with all your heart; do not depend on your own understanding. Seek his will in all you do, and he will show you which path to take" (Proverbs 3: 5–7 NLT).

CHAPTER 3

understanding Trauma

As adults, it takes courage and strength to sit down with someone safe and tell our stories when we are ready to heal. The healing process begins as we sort through the deep emotional and physical scars that have been left on our hearts and minds.

Holding back and pushing down a lifetime of pain and suffering from our consciousness only prolongs the inner battle. It's only a matter of time before the past starts to affect our physical health and relationships.

We suffer from migraines; our bodies start to ache; and our sleep is disturbed. Our bodies are carrying around unnecessary physical and mental weight. We wake up in the middle of the night sweating and with our hearts racing. We see dark images in our dreams, and we wonder what they mean. When the new day dawns, we remind ourselves we are safe now.

During the course of our day, at work or in public places, we smile even when it doesn't feel right, and we shake people's hands pretending to be confident when deep down inside we feel fearful. We strive to take back our physical health only to feel like we are going in circles and making zero progress.

Trauma is trapped in our bodies, and we don't know what to do in order to release it.

From my personal experience, I have learned healing requires more than simply telling my story, although telling the truth is helpful. I have had to find ways to relax my body and prevent re-triggering while my body tries to recover from the effects of trauma.

For survivors of trauma, the search for relief is constant. Each survivor must embrace the process with patience. It takes time, persistence, stumbling, setbacks, and sometimes crawling to reach the finish line of healing.

Memories

On the inside of my right arm above my wrist, there is a scar about four inches long, and on the same hand I have four other small scars. All these scars came from the same event when I was around age seven or eight, but I can't remember exactly what happened. When I try to remember, I feel it had something to do with broken glass.

That vague memory is how trauma works in most people's lives. We know that something happened to us, but we can't get a clear picture or explain it to anyone.

I have been left with deep physical and emotional scars. As I have walked through the healing from my trauma, I learned that I have both visible and invisible scars—and I can't remember the cause of most of them. Bits and pieces are coming back to me, and as the memories come, I share them with people I trust and who understand trauma and healing.

We all have some sort of story to tell. Some are good and some are sad to hear. Trauma affected me physically and mentally since I was a small child. I could not make sense of my story or describe how I felt on the inside. All my energy as a kid was put into making it through the next day. Sometimes I worried about whether my dad was going to come home drunk and angry. Other times I felt nervous if we had to go visit my dad in a mental hospital or prison. My body and mind were locked up and full of tension, racing with anxiety about the next event that would take place inside our family home. There was always something. I still have memories popping up here and there, but now I live in God's strength and grace to walk through the memories.

Having the power of God in my heart doesn't mean I don't feel the memories as they come. The pain and trauma are real. However, instead of remembering with my hands balled up in fists and my arms out of control, I am able to trust God with my pain and my healing.

My Reality

One day while I was in my basement folding laundry, these words came to me. I ran upstairs to write them down. I would like to share them with you because I believe it's very healing to get your feelings out in whatever form works for you. Just remember when we express how we feel we don't do it to hurt other people but to heal. I remember this particular day I was struggling with my binge eating and purging, and I was asking God to show me why I kept running back to this behavior.

Dear Daddy,
I'm 15 years old, pregnant, and I got jumped into my first gang,
but yet there's something inside of me that still wants you to love
me, protect me, and provide for me. I'm here today visiting you in
prison because you are locked up for ten years. I will never forget
the words you spoke to me when you saw me for the first time. You
were excited to show me the tattoo that you got on your arm of the
prison you were in. It showed the dates of your time served, which
were years you could have spent with me. When you finally stopped
talking enough to realize I was pregnant, you spoke the words to
me that I will never forget, "protect your body." What little did you
know this would keep your daughter bound to an eating disorder
for the next twenty years?

Even though I was about to give birth to my first child at the age fifteen, I was still yearning to be loved and accepted by my father. That day in my laundry room, God was showing me that the reason I keep hurting myself with food patterns is because I was trying to numb myself from the emptiness and pain the little girl inside of me was feeling.

When I was twenty-one years old, and I had given birth to my third child, and once again I longed for my dad to be a part of it. By this time he was out of prison but now he was in a psychiatric hospital. I wanted to introduce my son to my father. But for me to do that, I would have to visit him in the hospital in the psychiatric ward. I had to sit in the visitors' room and wait for him to be called out. As soon as I saw him walking towards me he seemed to be moving in very slow motion. He was in his hospital outfit, and he seemed to be heavily medicated. As he sat next to me, I handed him his grandson and noticed he was drooling from his mouth. He immediately started to pet my son like he was a dog.

When the first drop of saliva landed on top of my son's head, I knew this wasn't right, but I just sat there because I did not know how to respond. Everything inside of me felt like it was screaming, but once again I found myself sitting in silence and utter confusion.

All these experiences built a hard wall around me. I thought, *I will prove to you that I will be free from all this madness.* At age eighteen, I moved out on my own with the help of Section 8 housing and the welfare system. Even though I was already a parent of two small children, I harbored a desire to get approval and love from my parents.

I held onto the hope that one day my parents would change, and we would have a normal relationship. I felt immense pain but I couldn't break free. Instead, I went back only to find more pain.

Memories of trauma bring mixed emotions as they start to surface. Every survivor needs to talk to a trained trauma therapist who understands or find a person whom you feel comfortable with, but be sure that this person has walked through his or her healing process and that he or she is in a healthy state of mind and know Jesus and His word.

I have often wondered whether how I was feeling was right or wrong. I desired to have a healthy relationship with my parents, but in return I felt bad about myself, or I was left with confusion wondering if I expected too much from them. I needed to be reminded that what I desired as a child and as an adult was okay and healthy. My therapist and mentor helped me understand that in order to feel secure in our adult life, we needed to have love and stability at home as a child.

Memories can be tricky—and vague. We feel part of an event, but we can't remember the details. I often question myself—*was that really me, or am I making this up?* Trauma survivors protect themselves with fuzzy memories. But the way trauma survivors process memories varies with each individual. I am sharing my experience to encourage you in your journey, but that doesn't mean you will have the exact experience. I have purposely stayed away from trauma statistics in this chapter because I want to share from the heart of one trauma survivor to another.

I never heard the word trauma until I was in my mid-thirties. At that time, I didn't understand that I was living in a cycle of repeating patterns—a struggle that didn't make my life any easier.

I felt isolated and separated from the world. I could not relate to others, and I didn't have the words to express how I felt.

In the last chapter, I shared my journey of having to move away because distance is what I needed to begin healing. I had to separate myself for a season in order for my brain to process all I had been through. My body cried out for help, and I felt as if I was having a nervous breakdown. My eating disorder spiraled out of control. If I had not walked away from the toxic environment, I do not believe I would have been able to get the necessary help for my trauma.

In the fall of 2013, I found myself sitting in the office of a trauma therapist. When I had scheduled my appointment, I didn't know she specialized in trauma. I picked her because her website stated that she helped women with eating disorders. My binge eating and purging behaviors were uncontrollable. My body was in a constant state of anxiety.

At the time, I was newly married to my third husband, and I knew if I didn't get help this time, this wasn't going to be a good marriage either. By that time, I had a lot of healing and recovery under my belt but I had never dealt with my past issues.

Healing from trauma is not easy. That is why so many people spend their entire lives finding other ways to escape their pain.

Dissociation

Until I was able to get some relief from my trauma, I felt like I was in the world but living in a coma at the same time. Everything around me was moving, and my limp body just moved along with it. I disassociated all the time, and I wasn't even sure why I isolated myself.

I learned about dissociative identity disorder from my mentor who had experienced trauma, and my therapist talked to me about it as well. Dissociation is a common effect among people with early childhood trauma. The most common cause is extreme, repeated physical, sexual, and/or emotional abuse.

Dissociation is a disconnection between a person's thoughts, memories, feelings, and actions and the sense of who he or she is. When a person dissociates, he or she loses touch with awareness of their immediate surroundings.

Understanding this disorder filled me with relief. I had believed I was stupid, because I could not learn in school, couldn't remember people's names, and could not focus on conversations. My mind zoned out—I had no control over it and was not doing it on purpose.

My oldest son used to scream at me when he was a child, "You are not listening to me!" He would play tricks on me and tell me something and then repeat it and say something totally different just to see if I was listening. I felt extremely bad about myself because of this issue.

When I learned that zoning out was not my fault and was all due to my trauma, I felt hope and peace. At work, I carried a notepad with me to write down what someone said or what they asked me to do. The habit of writing every detail helped me keep my job and also helped me hide my struggle.

I still practice this habit today. If I hear a word I cannot pronounce or say, I will ask my husband, children, or a trusted friend.

The deeper I got into my trauma therapy, the more I realized the feelings of being in a coma were going away. I was able to have normal conversations where I listened without my head spinning. I noticed that I felt more present and wasn't so scared all the time around people.

And the last blessing was I started to enjoy the simplicity of life, like having a normal conversation and enjoying the birds, trees, and flowers. For so long I couldn't enjoy creation because my mind was trapped by all the trauma.

Survival Skills

In elementary school, I fell behind because I couldn't learn and keep up with other students. Believe me, I tried to listen to my teacher but my mind kept zoning out and all I heard was *wah, wah, wah.* When I was in middle school, my education declined fast, and other students started to notice that I couldn't learn. Due to all my anger and locked up emotions, feeling stupid, and not knowing what was wrong with me, I began acting out. I behaved badly to get kicked out of the classroom. *As long as I didn't have to stay in there and do work I couldn't do.*

Some days, they put me in an in-house suspension room, which is a room of isolation with a desk and four high walls to stare at for the entire school day. More time to think about my issues. In this little isolated room is where I had a lot of time to think about things I could do in order to cope with my life. When I would get out of school, I ran straight to the streets to find friends and people who would help me get high. There was even a neighbor guy who would let me come in his home and he would provide me with the skills and drugs to smoke crystal meth.

I didn't know how to express what I was feeling. I grew tired of it all. *Why am I so different from everybody else? Other students have nice clothes, play sports, go to school dances, and have no trouble getting their schoolwork done. I don't understand. What have I done to be like this?*

As the thoughts raced through my mind, I used my pencil eraser to make burn marks on my arms and legs. When I got really bored or felt as if I was going crazy, I carved words into my legs by using the little metal piece that is attached to the eraser of the pencil. During this time my dad was in prison, and my mom was never home. She was at work or stayed at the casinos for long nights of gambling.

One day in the seventh grade, I was walking down the hall and a girl bumped into me and said something that was not very nice. Next thing you know I lost it—dropped my books and started going crazy on her. I don't know any other way to explain it. I grabbed her by the hair and started punching her without stopping. It took about four teachers to get me off of her.

You may think, *what is wrong with her?* But when kids are confused and full of childhood trauma and anger, they need an outlet. They need someone who cares, someone who understands what they are going through. I believe this pent up anger is why there are so many school shootings and high gang activity.

A lot of my friends died from gang violence while growing up in Las Vegas. I was initiated into a gang at fifteen years old. My father was shot and lived, the brother of the father of my three children was murdered—trauma after trauma. So I speak from experience. When kids are filled with anger and confusion, they don't care about their lives or anybody else's. When I was living this way, I wanted help, but didn't know how to ask for it.

You have no idea the heaviness that left my body the day that I was able to tell my therapist how I felt as a child.

When she said, "It wasn't your fault," a new feeling came over me.

I asked, "Please tell me more, what do you mean?" *The words you are stupid and something is wrong with you have kept me imprisoned and living in fear my entire life.* I said, "Of course it was my fault that I couldn't learn!"

She repeated, "It was not your fault."

She explained how trauma victims dissociate in order to protect themselves. This idea took a while to sink in, but the loving people in my life like my husband, my spiritual mom, and my mentor, helped me to grasp this part of my story. I am still working on it. I am way behind on certain subjects. My three adult children, who have graduated from high school, will all be the first to tell you I was not able to help them with any homework past third grade level. But by the grace of God, they did extremely well in school.

It was the best feeling when I was able to make sense of my story and explain this part to my children. This is why I feel as trauma survivors we need to understand trauma, especially our own.

Instead of being ashamed, I started to become proud of who I had become. Instead of thinking I was stupid and couldn't learn, I started using my past experience as my strength. I have overcome my circumstances and shifted my mindset, and now my life is changed for the better.

If I had never used the gift of dissociation as a survival technique when I was young, I might not have been able to make it to adulthood.

Triggers

A trigger is when your past experiences interfere with your present living. A trigger interrupts life without any warning whatsoever. Sometimes you don't know you are being triggered, yet you have a rush of emotions such as fear and anger. Triggers are not good or bad, they are just signals given to our bodies to help protect us from harm or to let us know we are dealing with an emotion. When a trigger happens, be very patient with yourself, and do not beat yourself up for feeling like you are having an off day.

Trauma can be life controlling, and believe it or not, trauma is everywhere. People with trauma are sitting in classrooms, worshiping in church pews, reporting to nine-to-five jobs sitting behind a desk, holding job titles like CEO, and more.

Trauma can leave you feeling helpless. In some counseling appointments, nothing seemed to help me. We talked about the current behaviors and patterns and where I felt stuck, but we never tapped into my past. Oftentimes I was given a Bible verse to go home and memorize, but as much as I love the Word of God now, a Bible verse in the midst of trauma isn't always helpful.

Some therapists made promises such as, "Jesus will make all your pain go away." The truth is that sometimes He does in this life and sometimes He doesn't. I've witnessed people having their relationships restored with those who abused them and living happily ever after, but that kind of healing wasn't my case with my mother and father. Instead, I had to keep up strong boundaries to protect my heart and to prevent constantly being re-triggered.

But it's important to know that the pain we feel and the trauma we have experienced is not a life sentence and does not have to control us for the rest of our lives. No traumatic experience is too much for God to handle. It may be hard to work through, even with the help of Jesus, but it takes patience and trusting that God has a plan even in the midst of our suffering and losses.

I've been in my healing journey for years now, and I can still get very uncomfortable around certain people or places. It's not that I am afraid of them—more like I choose not to be around certain people or places today. A certain person might remind me of someone from when I was growing up. Or a place with heavy drinking or noise makes me feel uneasy. I'm not condemning all drinking of alcohol because I know some people can enjoy one or two drinks. But I must be sensitive to the environments I put myself in. If not, my mind can drift into some really dark places, and I will want to shut down. This is how I know that the environment is affecting me, and I usually limit my time there and get to a place where I know I can relax and take care of myself.

When you have experienced a lot of trauma—or any trauma at all—it is very important to guard your thoughts and recognize how you feel when you leave certain places. I remind myself daily that I have the mind of Christ (1 Corinthians 2:16) and to take every negative thought captive (2 Corinthians 10:5).

My mind can play crazy tricks on me because of my upbringing. It still wants me to believe that I am different from everybody else. That I am unlovable. It whispers *nobody likes you* and *you have nothing good to say*. It likes to keep me silent and tells me, *you shouldn't say that* or *you didn't do that right*. It even tries to control what I wear. It tries to convince me I am not worthy.

I feel it's important for me to be honest with you about this, because once I got my heart healed, I then had to work extremely hard on reprogramming my mind. The Bible tells us that we have the mind of Christ and that we are created in his image. There is nothing wrong with you; it's only your experiences that try to make you believe there is. My childhood experiences could have ruined my life, and this has happened to many people. A horrific incident happens, then they never tell anybody, and it affects their entire life.

My hope every day when I share my message is that people will find the courage to open up about their experiences and no longer hide in shame believing they did something wrong. A Bible verse written by Paul while he was in jail explains how God wants us to think.

"Finally, brothers and sisters, whatever is true, whatever is noble, whatever is right, whatever is pure, whatever is lovely, whatever is admirable—if anything is excellent or praiseworthy—think about such things" (Philippians 4:8 NIV).

You do not have to live with the effects of your trauma for the rest of your life. You can have a peaceful and successful life. You are capable of learning how to handle triggers when they come up—without losing your self-control. Yes, trauma is hard to overcome, and it hurts. But it is one hundred percent possible to get to the place where you can talk about it and not be affected by your old emotions.

Pain Is Not The End Of Your Story

When I was going through my trauma therapy, there were many days when I came home, wrapped myself in a blanket, and followed up with a nice bubble bath. Other days I wanted to play, so I would call up a friend and ask them to go have lunch with me and maybe do some shopping.

I had to learn, as a survivor of childhood trauma, that I was worthy of love even though I had never received love. It was okay to create the experience of intimate closeness I so desperately needed as a child.

It's important to forgive others—and yourself. Forgiveness frees us from oppression and depression and releases us from the bonds that tie us to our pain.

Everything that I have been through in life I can now say has been a teaching opportunity. I'm no longer ashamed of it. I am a stronger person because of my story. My experience lets me give others hope through my story of how trauma affected my life.

reflection

Our bodies were not made to live in a constant state of suffering. When we were created in our mother's womb, it was to live a life of joy and freedom.

As we weep, God weeps with us. There are many stories in the Bible where people cried out to God, "Where are you?"

1. Let God know exactly how you feel. It you can't put words to it, then tell Him you have no words. Ask Him to show you what needs to be dealt with so you can release more of the trauma that is in your body.

2. Don't be afraid to ask hard questions. "God where were you when this was happening to me? Help me understand why I had to go through something so terrible."

3. Now spend some time soaking in His presence with worship music or just silence. Maybe take a bath. And ask Him to show you the good in your suffering.

prayer

Dear God,
You know my heart. Something inside me desires change, but
to change I know I need to face my pain. Will you give me the
willingness and patience to face the trauma in my body that I have
never dealt with? In Jesus' name I pray. Amen

scripture

"The sacrifice you desire is a broken spirit. You will not reject a broken and repentant heart, O God" (Psalm 51: 17 NLT).

If you would like to read some stories of people who experienced trauma through family dysfunction please take some time to read the stories of Judah and Tamar, (*Genesis 38; and Amnon and Tamar, 2 Samuel 13*). These are awful stories among God's people, but He didn't intervene or prevent abuse from happening. These people were not given easy or quick recoveries, yet He still showed His love and power through their redemptive stories.

CHAPTER 4

no more protecting family secrets

As survivors, we often downplay what we went through even though our lives were filled with addiction, abuse, and neglect. We tell ourselves it wasn't that bad. But denial is temporary relief and does not face the pain of our reality.

Even though I am an adult, I still feel the little-girl fear inside of me. I may never be completely free of the pain I felt growing up in a home so broken. I constantly feared my father, who was an addict, but I also feared my mother, whose behavior was so unpredictable because she was addicted to my father.

Understanding my emotions, fear, and anxiety took a long time. When I had these feelings I dealt with them in the best way I knew how to at the time. I wasn't taught any proper coping skills. No one was there to prepare me.

I didn't know how to express the pain and torment, let alone understand myself. I felt stuck in not knowing what was wrong with me for a very long time. In middle school, I rushed home from school to sit alone in my bedroom and cut myself, making slashes on my legs and arms—desperately wanting somebody to notice the pain I felt. My body and mind felt out of control and full of confusion.

I picked up controlling behaviors at a young age, hoping this would give me some sort of power back in my life.

But what all these behaviors did was make me feel like I was going crazy. When I became an adult, these survival skills pushed people farther away from me. I was spinning in a cycle of obsessive-compulsive and codependent behaviors. I felt scared and alone.

When I became a mom, my behaviors worsened. I told my children what they could and could not do. Then I followed with a warning about all the mistakes I had made as I shared my pain from my past.

I never wanted to see one of my kids suffer or feel the pain I had felt as a child.

In my early twenties I had a long battle with an eating disorder that made me sick and consumed my life even though I kept it a secret. I couldn't stop my binge eating and purging behaviors.

After years of suffering, I learned that eating disorders are common among women who were raised by an addicted parent or who have been sexually abused. Compulsively controlling eating is another form of trying to control pain. Unfortunately, these issues are not popular topics, especially in religious settings. I made a promise to myself that I will share my struggle with whoever it might help.

I was also a workaholic who never knew how to slow down or relax. I worked and worked until my body hit a wall of exhaustion. I was suffering from an internal battle while trying to function like an adult in the real world.

I struggled with disassociation, a condition where a person disconnects from his or her true self. People who disassociate can't get in touch with their feelings. I disassociated because I had no clue what I was feeling. I wasn't sure if there was something wrong, and if there was, who could I talk to about it? I never told anyone, because I was still repressing memories from my childhood.

I had never heard the words *addiction* and *trauma* as a kid, even though I grew up surrounded by both. But this is a true story for many people. They don't realize their home environment was full of dysfunction and addiction until they start having problems in all their relationships or in marriage later in life.

I developed these same behaviors because I didn't understand my home situation. A person doesn't simply wake up one day and say, *I think I will become an addict, then cut myself and develop an eating disorder when I grow up. That sounds fun.* These behaviors result because something happened and led to becoming emotionally disturbed.

When you become aware of coping behaviors in your adult life and realize these behaviors are not healthy and are not keeping you safe, then it is time to let them go. I do not recommend doing this on your own or in your own strength. If I had tried that I would've probably hurt myself many times—or someone else.

While my coping behaviors gave me some temporary relief from pain, fear, and anxiety, some were destroying my life in a toxic way. I needed God's help to let go of them, and I needed the help of my mentor who held me accountable and never abandoned me when I needed emotional support—especially in the area of my eating disorder.

When I faced a trigger, it was as if my old coping behaviors would pop up and say, "*Use me, I'm here if you still need me.*" Promising to make me feel better and relieve some of my pain.

My brain needed some serious rewiring, and I needed God to show me how to let go and trust him instead of my old behaviors. And I had to have many tools put in place to help me recover, such as resting and allowing myself to get centered and calm enough to get in touch with what I was actually feeling.

Nothing was ever going to change in my life until I could muster up the courage to look at what had actually happened to me. I knew I needed help and something was seriously wrong. In my late thirties, I had a nervous breakdown. I hit rock bottom. My body could no longer function, and I could no longer bury the pain from all the trauma I had endured. And I didn't want to keep living that way. I was exhausted.

Overworking, cutting myself, binge eating and purging, constant fear and anxiety, and trying to control everything led to fatigue and depression.

When we start speaking the truth of what really happened, it will be scary at first. It took every living breath inside of me to stop justifying what had happened to me and to turn off the belief system my childhood wasn't that bad. I thought if I talked about how I really felt, I was a weak person, and I was betraying my family. *Who wants to say their parents did things they shouldn't have?* But the reality of opening up to others is the opposite. Only a strong person admits the truth and faces his or her pain.

It took a lot of years in recovery and therapy and a lot of talking about myself to truly understand all that I went through as a child. Sometimes I blamed myself—*I should have been tougher or I need to quit complaining about my childhood.*

When I began my healing journey I could not pinpoint one event to my therapist because a series of events had wounded me deeply.

A person doesn't snap out of trauma because trauma is rooted in your tissues and bones until you address the original cause of it. After all these years, I have learned that any behavior that prolongs the recovery and healing process means I am not willing to look at the truth of what happened. We cannot be set free from the pain we have suffered ... or may still be suffering until we face our pain with honesty.

The Heart of a Broken Child

Most childhood trauma survivors get stuck when they start having painful memories because they feel overwhelmed, or they second-guess whether their memories are true. Often, turning to addiction numbs their pain, because facing the reality of what their truth might be can be painful.

Imagine a little child who is helpless and who you deeply love and care about. Maybe your children or a niece or nephew. Maybe you are to a point that you can see yourself as a child. Whoever it is, I want you to imagine them when I share a story with you. Now if the child you are thinking about had to experience some of the situations I am going to describe, I would like you to take a minute and ask yourself these questions. Maybe even journal what comes to you.

1. How does it make you feel? Angry? Sad?

2. How would you handle the situation?

3. Would you tell yourself what this child has been through is really not that bad and they need to just get over it?

I am not going to use the word *boy* or *girl* when referring to this child, because I want you to envision the child you are choosing to think about. Just trust the process and stay with me.

There was a child who grew up in a home filled with violence and addiction. This child's father struggled with drugs and alcohol. Most of the time when he was under the influence, he became violent toward his family, even the small child. The mother was always preoccupied with the father, trying to keep the peace, and she was not capable of providing the time this child so desperately needed from her. The mother allowed this behavior to go on, never protecting the child from harm. This child started to live a life in constant fear because the child never knew what to expect next. Sometimes this child's father would disappear for months, and they never knew when he would be back home. Sometimes when he came home he would bring his girlfriend with him, even though he was a married man. There were times this child's father would come home so messed up on drugs that he would have to be rushed to the hospital and then be placed in the psychiatric ward to be cared for. The mother would leave the younger children home alone with an older sibling not older than age ten, or rush them to someone else's house to be cared for. When the child had to go visit the father, he would sometimes be slurring and slobbering due to all the medications he was on. At other times, this child would come home and the father would be cussing and throwing things at the child or mother for no apparent reason. This child was often left with other people to be cared for because of the father's addiction. Then another family member sexually abused this child.

The Stolen Identity of a Traumatized Child

Now pause for a moment … Sit with this for a while. Visualize all that this child has endured in his or her short lifetime. Was it okay? Would you say what this child has been through is really not that bad? Do you think this child might have some issues when he or she grows up? Is this a normal household? Do you think any child should have to experience this kind of behavior? What about you? Did you ever experience any of these situations?

Too many children are growing up in this type of family. But the problem is that most of them don't realize that their home life is not right or healthy. In this process, their identity is being destroyed. Years of their youth are being stolen by the fear and anxiety they feel. They can't focus at school because of what's going on at home. Most children downplay what they have been through because they feel it's their fault or they are trying to protect the family by keeping secrets. Many children are already learning at a young age how to shut down in order to survive.

I believe trauma in the home is a huge problem with our society. So many children are overly stressed and the strain is causing damage to their brains at young ages. Teachers are not equipped to recognize the signs of childhood trauma. Many adults are messed up from their past and struggle with some type of addiction or self-destructive behavior because no one recognizes that they need help.

When you are full of trauma, you don't know where to ask for proper help. And trauma memories don't come back for years—sometimes not until the person is an adult. By that time, if the abused victim tries to talk about it, people either think they are lying or will ignore that the abuse even happened. Sometimes the abuser has died.

The typical response from the abuse victim is to try to make the memories go away. First by telling themselves it really wasn't that bad and second by refusing to talk about it. The person stops searching for help. Some abuse victims even live with this secret while still trying to get the abuser to love them.

The only way to heal is to deal with what happened. If people don't get the help they need, they will stay wounded vessels who constantly wound other people. And parents will pass their wounds on to their children.

As a person who has endured trauma, it took a lot for me to admit I needed help. And I mean a lot. There were so many steps I had to take to get help so I could get where I am today. I left some people behind. I had to get desperate enough to go to any measure to find help. I was deeply affected; I had major mother and father wounds that were painful to face. To feel rejected by your parents or family is a hard injury to recover from.

If you've experienced some kind of abuse or neglect, it really is a big deal and your heart needs to be healed from it. I learned only God, my Creator, could heal that deepest part of me and return my true identity. I needed to be restored to the child who was never wounded. When I grasped what Jesus did for me on the cross, it was a huge game changer. He died for all of my sins, all the horrible actions I did and all the painful actions people did to me.

Remember, there are many stages to the healing process, and your pain doesn't go away overnight. To learn to forgive yourself and other people will take time. Just because we start to believe in God or become a Christian doesn't mean we come to Jesus and immediately forgive and forget. We first have to recognize and understand, possibly even get angry about, all that has happened.

As innocent children, we often carry the burden of our parent's addiction, believing we did something wrong to cause it. We try to come up with solutions— what we could have done differently to make them stop drinking and love us. Maybe if I clean my room better, or maybe if I speak less. But when these coping mechanisms don't work, we become full of self-hate and guilt, believing maybe if we were different then they would stop. That is a huge load for any child to carry. It leaves the child feeling afraid and alone.

In most homes with addiction, children are not allowed to talk or feel. But in the long run, children suffer. I would like you to know right now that no matter who you are or what you have done, **you are not responsible for another person's choices or behavior!**

When I was growing up in this type of environment, I wasn't aware there was another way of living. I just thought what I was going through was what all families went through. As young children, we relate to no one other than our families to comprehend the world around us.

As young as I can remember, around age five, I learned how to survive my upbringing and started to put into action what made me feel safe. But when I became an adult and tried to use the same survivor skills, these coping methods didn't work, mainly because I was still acting like a scared child. I had a lot to work on, including being in healthy relationships, boundaries (this was a big one), finances, my own addictions, and my poor habits. The emotions of having to face all these issues at once made me feel like I wanted to run into a hole and hide forever. But the people who helped me always reminded me to slow down and keep it simple. They helped me not to try to do it in my own strength but to ask God for help. There were a lot of real life activities I didn't know how to do, like cooking, proper hygiene, how to read, and how to interact with other people. I had completely shut down during my childhood years.

Survival Skills

God has given us the gift to block out certain memories at certain times of our lives. I know this may sound weird, but can you imagine having to deal with all your painful memories at one time? I don't think our minds could handle it.

Every time a child experiences something traumatic, he or she goes into a "fight or flee" mode in order to survive. Over time a child's developing brain is changed by these repeated traumatic experiences. Areas of the brain that govern the retention of memory, the regulation of emotion, and the development of language skills are affected. The result is a brain that has structurally adapted to survival under the most stressful circumstances—but not for success in the world.

The way I survived also became a huge problem later in life. I had a lot of catching up to do from all that I had blocked out in my life, especially what I was supposed to learn in school. There was no way my little brain could absorb anything at school because I was in a constant fight or flee mode, prepared for what was next. I was on guard at all times.

When I started to get really behind in school, I started to believe the lie that I must have been born this way. I thought I was born stupid. When I was in school sitting in a classroom I could not comprehend what they were teaching. Even though deep down inside I was hungry to learn, I could not explain the disconnect that was going on. Most of my teachers viewed me as a defiant student who didn't want to learn.

My teachers had no idea what was happening in my home life.

My parents weren't any help to me, because most of my trauma was coming from their choices. The only time my mom showed up at school was when I was in trouble.

Due to my brain shutting down because of the trauma, I was put into special classes at school—a self-esteem crusher that made a huge impact on the types of friends I chose. I was for sure not going to hang around smart kids who played sports. First of all I didn't feel worthy enough.

For the longest time, I operated as a broken child who was still scared, and my brain was developmentally delayed. Not being able to read as an adult was one of the most embarrassing things I had to overcome, and it's still hard today. I still get corrected on how I pronounce certain words. It caused me to think very poorly of myself at times. But today I now see myself as a fighter who was not willing to give up and lie down and accept what life was scripting for me. Has it been hard at times? Yes! Have I wanted to give up? Yes! But if I did, how would I be able to share my message that there is a way out.

I had to pass up jobs because of my lack of education. I often wondered what it would be like to be a secretary. I remember as a little girl any time I could get my hands on a typewriter or keyboard I would type away, pushing many buttons really believing I was writing something. Now look at me today writing a book and deeply motivated to inspire others who are still hurting from the effects of trauma.

God had a plan all along for my life and your life, too, since the day we were born. Does His plan mean we will never experience pain again?

Absolutely not. This world is full of pain and hurting people, so there is a pretty big chance we will. But some have to go through a lot more pain than others. But know that the deeper level of your pain, the deeper message you have to share with the world.

When we let Jesus who has overcome death and sin rule in our lives and write the next chapters of our lives, something magical takes place— if we are willing to trust and push past our pain, fear, and doubts, because on a healing journey there will be many.

I'm not trying to get all churchy with you. Believe me, when I was hurting and all messed up, I hated it when people would say churchy stuff to me. But when I learned who God is and started to talk to Him about everything—how I was feeling, what I was afraid of, what I was angry about—my life started to shift for the better.

For a long time I couldn't hold a conversation with most people because of all my brokenness. I couldn't look people in the eyes because of my guilt, shame, and secrets. I hope my vulnerability motivates you to take a closer look at your life. Are you missing out on life because of your past? Could you do more with your life if you took some time to heal and work on yourself?

When I started to realize there was a block holding me back from living my life and learning, I was on a mission to find out what it was. And after spending years searching, I realized it was my pain from childhood and brokenness that stopped me from living my life to its full potential. My identity had been shattered into countless pieces. It took something much bigger than human power for me to be restored.

Who God created me to be was torn apart by those closest to me. The ones I called my family. This pain I had suffered caused a lot of my problems in life, like preventing me from learning how to read or to love myself. I had major anxiety attacks, followed up with many sleepless nights. I stayed way too long in multiple abusive relationships. With all the other things I struggled with, I constantly felt bound by a rope that I could not untangle. I was taking one step forward and three steps backward.

But someone told me that there is an enemy who is out to destroy my life. It's his goal to kill, steal, and accuse me, and he wants me to stay stuck this way forever. He loves to steal people's identities through abuse and neglect. But we also need to understand that Jesus came to set us free and heal our broken hearts.

Remember I said I was willing to go to any measure to get free. I started asking a lot more questions about Jesus and what He had to offer. I was hungry to learn about God and the power I could have in His son Jesus. The more I learned of God's plan for my life, it empowered me to want to break free from this old pattern that was getting me nowhere in life. It was only holding me back from the life I deserved.

I had to admit that what I went through as a child really *was* that bad. I had to let God in on the deepest secrets I never shared with anyone—all my struggles and pain. I had to talk to Him about my fear. I had to learn to be gentle with myself with all my ups and downs through the process. And while going through this, I had to learn to put up healthy boundaries by saying no to people so I could get the help I needed.

My faith played a huge role in my healing process and my recovery program. Both my faith and recovery encouraged me to keep going and to never give up on myself. Like I shared in Chapter One, when I heard the scripture Jeremiah 29:11, it prompted something in me to start asking questions and to start moving forward with action. The verse states as follows, "'For I know the plans I have for you,' says the LORD. 'They are plans for good and not for disaster, to give you a future and a hope.'"

Well, that is exactly what I wanted. I wanted a future and I needed hope. I wanted out of the current life I was living. I wanted to get far away from drugs, alcohol, and abuse, and I for sure wanted my kids away from it.

The more help that I got, the braver I became. And the stronger I got, the more changes I was able to make to better my life. I will never forget the day I told myself *you can learn to read*. The next step I took was walking into Walmart and purchasing a spell checker and dictionary all-in-one calculator. It was almost twenty years ago.

I became determined to teach myself how to read. This became one of my new favorite tools over the next ten years. Instead of saying *I can't read* or *I don't know how*, I started to teach myself new words every day.

The more I healed, the more determined I was to become the woman God created me to be. Over time I felt like my brain was starting to work again. I felt like I was coming out of a coma. I was becoming alive again and finding my true self. I no longer had to shut down all the time, because I was finding my voice and learning to discern what I needed in life. I became like a sponge, soaking up any information that I could get my hands on. I was so hungry to study, and I was willing and ready to do anything to learn all I had missed out on. I am still learning and growing. And I am very proud about it! I no longer hide behind a coat of shame. If I hear a word that I don't know, you better believe I will ask the person to repeat it.

reflection

Clinical research has shown that childhood trauma and neglect are stored in the tissue of the child, and the emotional or physical trauma does not go away until an effort is made to address the original cause.

1. Why are you reading this book? What do you need to address in your life?

2. How was your childhood? Ask God to show you if there are any hidden issues that haven't been dealt with.

3. Have you been running for a long time from a particular situation and telling yourself it wasn't that bad? If so, how is it affecting your life today?

prayer

Dear God,
I come to you very broken and confused. I feel something is holding
me back in life, and I'm not sure what it is. Please show me what
I've been afraid to deal with. Have I been talking myself out of the
pain by saying it wasn't that bad? I am trusting you to show me
if I have not dealt with trauma that is wounding my soul. I am

inviting you into those secret dark places and memories that are still holding me bound. I know that you are the God who heals, and nothing I share with you will stop you from loving me. Amen.

scripture

"And you will know the truth, and the truth will set you free"
(John 8:32 NLT).

CHAPTER 5

victim of our circumstances

*Children become victims of their circumstances—sometimes
without realizing it—when parents or role models choose to hide
their pain with addiction, or when a parent takes their anger out
on the child. Their lives become difficult without even knowing it,
until they are old enough to recognize the trauma they have been
through, and find the help to start to unravel it.*

What does it mean to become a victim of our circumstances? As I walk you through this chapter, I hope you will find a better understanding of some of the struggles you might be hanging onto from your childhood. When we become victims unaware, it's hard to discern what's our fault and what's not. We take blame for what we had no control over. Becoming unstuck helps us heal from the deep scars. Maybe your experiences as a young child are still affecting your life today in some way. Unhealed trauma causes problems in our finances, health, and can even affect your relationships because it's hard to get along with other people.

Personally, I wrestled with my past a lot longer than I would have liked. For the longest time, I could not connect my unresolved childhood issues with my adult problems. I had no idea how my difficulties or my sicknesses were connected to growing up in addiction. But they were. Through the sharing of my struggles, I hope to shed some light on situations you may be dealing with right now. We can't get free until we identify the struggle and then get to the source of what is causing it. I know it sounds simple, but too many people stay stuck in this battle.

The effects of verbal and emotional abuse are hard to comprehend when we are children, especially when we don't know how to challenge it. If we were told repeatedly as small children that we were stupid, ugly, unlovable, and worthless, these words will stick with us and as adults and the negative voices become the recording that plays in our head—until we acknowledge that it was abuse. We become imprisoned by the words that were spoken over us again and again, and they begin to define our identity and control our actions. The process begins with learning to grieve the loss we felt as children because we heard these harsh words spoken to us by those we loved and wanted to protect us. If we don't take the time to grieve it, the rejection will become our core belief system, stealing our joy and self-worth. There are tools that can help us and build our desire to combat the lies with truth.

What helped me to uproot some of these lies was spending time studying God's Word until it became my new truth and spending time with people who loved me. I needed safe people to speak into my life until I could believe my worth for myself. My spiritual mom who was like a mom to me often spoke these words: "You have always been enough since the day you were born."

People who grow up in a toxic or poverty environment struggle. Research shows it affects mind, body, and soul, creating emotional and social distress. Many children who have grown up in poverty also have been traumatized in many ways. According to Eric Jensen in his book *Poor Students, Rich Teaching*, the number of children living in poverty who have been traumatized has been estimated between 50 percent and 80 percent. When children go without food, they start to believe it's their fault, and they deserve it. Children start to think *maybe it's because I was bad.*

I was traumatized over and over again as a child. For the first 18 years of my life my family had 6,570 days to shame me and expose me to dysfunction. When children grow up this way how can they not be affected by it?

When I was in the seventh grade, I often came home to an empty house—with no food. My mother struggled with her gambling addiction and didn't come home for long periods of time. Her absence left me to care for my little brother.

When we were hungry I would run to the casino where I knew I could find her most of the time. Even though it was often dark, I learned what back alleys to run through to try to get there as quick as I could. I remember how happy I was when found a street that had more streetlights. I was scared to go there alone, but I knew this was the only way my brother and I were going to eat.

At the casino I would dart across the parking lot, heading straight toward the side doors where a bowling alley was attached. Something made me feel safe about walking through there first. Maybe it's because I knew teenagers hung out there, and it was nice to see kids like myself before I had to walk into the casino area where the slot machines were. I started looking for mom by looking at the backs of people's heads. Sometimes I found her right away, and sometimes it took a while. I can still smell the smoke from the cigarettes filling the atmosphere and hear the change dropping from all the slot machines.

These experiences taught me at a young age how to become a survivor, especially during my school years. The more trauma I endured, the harder my heart became and the better I got at zoning out my fears and numbing myself for the next thing that would happen in my life. Surviving is how I learned to prepare myself and be ready for the next crisis.

I often wonder what might have happened if someone had recognized that I was a young child being raised in a home where my father was a raging alcoholic who controlled his children through fear and intimidation. I wonder if someone could've stepped in made a difference. His choices eventually sent him to prison, leaving my mother a single mom of six children. When she couldn't take the pressure of being a single mom any longer, she escaped through her addiction, spending long nights and days at the casino.

If we could somehow identify children who are hurting and under a lot of stress, we could be that helping hand to children who were once like me by helping them relieve that stress in healthy ways or meeting some of their needs. I remember every teacher who tried to reach out to me. I don't know for sure, but maybe they suspected something was wrong. What an impact schools could make in a child's life if staff were offered more training on how to recognize childhood trauma. If you see a child in distress don't be afraid to say, "How are you today?" Ask if they need something to eat or someone to talk to or a safe place to calm down for a minute. For some children, school is the only safe place they have to go. I always laid my head on the desk and fell asleep when I got to school.

I was so tired because there was no structure at home. Sometimes all these children need is someone to show them they care. Too often these children are viewed as hopeless and trust me that is so far from the *truth*.

We are only in the beginning of this chapter, but I want to ask you a question, and I am going to be straightforward. Do you have any childhood wounds that you haven't dealt with? Are you satisfied with how your life has turned out so far? Has your life or that of someone you know been affected in any way by trauma and addiction? Take a minute and look back over your life. Do you feel there is anything currently holding you back from the life you desire to live? It can be helpful to journal your answers. If you are a believer in Christ Jesus, ask Him to show you if there is any area where you need to be healed. Your load of heaviness, shame, and guilt is not yours to carry. Shame can keep people trapped in a pattern of confusion, self-hate, and self-destructive patterns. Get help to get unstuck. Find a safe place to express all the hurts and fears you have kept inside, and free yourself from the shame that was never yours to carry in the first place. My mentor always says it's okay to take off your coat of shame.

I was trapped in a vicious cycle of binge eating and purging for a long time. I hated this cycle, and I wanted to be free. When I was struggling or when I was filled with shame for binge eating, I would call my spiritual mom, the one who would remind me that I was lovable and enough since the day I was born. She always answered my phone calls, something I wasn't used to. I would cry and tell her I was struggling with my eating disorder and she'd respond. "Paula this isn't about food but it is about the pain you are carrying." I could never understand why she always repeated this to me, and to be honest, her words used to make me angry sometimes. But what I finally learned was the freedom to speak about what I went through as a child without being judged or shut down for the first time in my life. The day I could finally be honest with someone and share my story and tell them that my dad was an addict and abusive felt like a weight was being lifted. For the longest time, there were so many secrets. It took a long time for me to finally open up to someone. You will hear me often refer to my spiritual mom in this book. Her name is Cat. I met her at my first 12-step recovery meeting when I was 24 years old. She came up to me after a meeting and gave me her business card. It was hard at first to pick up the phone to call her but after I did, we spent months on the phone that turned into years. It wasn't just *a one time share my story, and it was over with* kind of deal. It took time to even be able to get to the point to describe to her what I was feeling and how my upbringing affected me. That's why I repeat myself by saying healing is a process and to not give up. It hurts me to see so many people give up because they think they will never heal.

When I continued to work through my childhood issues it didn't take long for me to realize *wow, the guy I am with behaves just like my dad,* this was a huge wake-up. I needed healthy people in my life to tell me I didn't have to live like this anymore. I needed someone to explain it was abuse. I needed someone to hold my hand and tell me I didn't have to be physically abused and cursed out anymore. Because that was all I saw growing up, that is what I thought I deserved. Not only that, it was scary to believe for anything good in my life. But when loving people kept reassuring me, I became stronger and stronger.

When we become adults, we become responsible for how we want to show up in the world. We must be careful who we ask for help because some people can do more damage if they don't know how to help someone who has experienced severe trauma. Work with someone who can understand you, your story, and help you walk through it all. Once we start working through all our pain, fear, and shame, we can give ourselves the gift of life, by living happy and free. Giving our self what was stolen from us as a child, such as true identity, love, nurture, and a safe place to live. This process takes work, but it brings a lot of healing and comfort.

Share Your Story So Others Can Find Healing

One night as I went to my recovery meeting—which is where I go when I need extra support, besides spending time with God—there was a little girl about age eleven who walked in with an older couple who appeared to be married. In this particular meeting each person is given a chance to share why they are there. I remember wondering what brought this child to the meeting.

When the gentleman who was with her spoke, he shared that his daughter was an alcoholic and that the little girl was his granddaughter.

The granddaughter was living with him, so he could help raise her and try to protect her from her mother. The mother drove with the child in the car while she was drunk and often provoked verbal altercations with the child.

Next it was the little girl's turn to speak. Her soft voice came across the room. "My mommy drinks all the time. Now she is in a detox program."

The moment she started speaking, I got a lump in my throat and my eyes filled with tears. *What is it about this little girl that is touching me?* I was so grateful I had spoken before her, because I don't think I would've been able to speak without crying. The next week she was there again— right next to an open chair. I sat by her. This time her grandma brought her to the meeting. As usual, everyone went around the room sharing what was on their hearts. When it got to her grandma, she decided to pass. "I will just listen tonight."

Then the little girl spoke with bravery in her voice, "I come to these meetings because my mommy drinks."

The moment I heard her words something hit me smack dab in the middle of my heart, and I felt that familiar lump in my throat again. Now it was my turn to speak, and all eyes were on me. Everyone was waiting. Tears filled my eyes. *What am I going to say? What will everyone think?* I sat silent.

I heard the Holy Spirit whisper, *it's okay to share what's on your heart, and how you are feeling.*

I took a deep breath, and I gently put my hand on the little girl's back. I didn't use big words; instead I tried to remember how I felt when I was her age and what would you have wanted someone to tell you. Emotions stirred inside of me. I looked at her with a smile and we locked eyes immediately. I said, "If anyone gets what you are going through, I do."

Her head then moved in a little closer to hear what I had to say.

"You remind me of me when I was your age, and all I wanted was for my parents to love me. I was very scared and confused and my body was going through a lot of changes. I remember thinking it was my fault that my dad was drinking or using drugs or when my mom didn't come home at night. For a long time I took full responsibility that I needed to fix my parents, or thought maybe if I changed, they would change, too."

I then shared that it wasn't until later that I learned that my parents were sick, and they were not capable of giving me the love and attention that I deserved. I then looked at her grandma and said, "I am so glad you have your grandma to take care of you." I followed it up with, "It's okay to be sad on days when you miss your mom. I still miss my parents to this day." But I asked her to try to do one thing for me, and that was to try to focus on being a little girl and having fun with her friends.

When we grow up in addiction or dysfunction, we find little time to play. When we are faced with adult chaos and adult decisions at a young age, we kick into survival mode.

The little girl touched a sensitive place in my soul, but it also reminded me of why I keep sharing my story and why I want to write this book, so I can let others know they are not alone and no one has to walk this journey alone. We can heal from the brokenness of childhood. We don't have to like our experience, but we do have to learn to accept it and heal from it. Sharing our story and our pain with someone who understands is how we heal. When someone says, "I'm sorry you are going through this, I went through it, too," the words and the empathy offer hope. People need to know they can heal and overcome, and they need to know they don't have to do it alone. It's okay to admit we are broken and that we want help. Too many people live with unnecessary pain because they won't admit they are suffering.

It's okay to not be okay. We try to cover it up with perfectionism, people pleasing, and approval seeking. Some of us even fall victim to addiction.

We live with so much pain in our hearts, and we start to believe that life can't get better. People often believe *this must be my lot in life*. I want you to know if you admit your brokenness before Jesus and cry out from the depths of your heart, and share your pain, your weaknesses, and your struggles, He is there waiting for you. Jesus can heal any wound because He understands our pain. He has been there, too. He died a brutal death to set us free.

You may say, "I don't know how to talk to God." Well, it is more simple than you think. You talk to Him just like you would a trusted friend. You don't change the way you look, or the way you stand, or your voice tone. Just open your mouth and speak out whatever is on your heart at the time. If you don't know what to say, just say the name of Jesus, or *Jesus, I know things aren't supposed to be this way.*

I spent a lot of years self-destructing because I felt the pain was unbearable. I was stuck in a vicious cycle of not knowing how to feel and being scared to feel the pain. I once heard that the only way to heal was to feel the pain and to remember even though it may hurt, that pain is not going to destroy you. I remember thinking, *okay, this cycle is getting old, and it is getting me nowhere.* I would feel pain or emotions, then I would use my addiction to cope, then this started a pattern of feeling guilty, full of shame, sick, and depressed.

I wanted to face the pain head on. To do that, I had to let go of people and my will. I went through a season of feeling very depressed and heavy-hearted. In this season I stayed close to God, my mentor, and my recovery program. God puts the right people in our path—people that we need at the time.

Some days I am reminded of the pain that has come from my family of origin and growing up in addiction and dysfunction. When I see other women my age posting pictures on social media of themselves with their mom, or if I'm at a sporting event and I see grandparents cheering their grandchildren, it makes my heart hurt because these are experiences I will never have. Even the holidays are painful for me, because everyone is getting together with their families. I often struggle with thinking, *Was there anything I could have done differently to spend more time with my parents?* But I know there was nothing I could have done differently to change my circumstances or upbringing.

My recovery program and the people I choose to surround myself with today remind me all the time: "You didn't cause it." "It's not your job to fix it." "You can't control other people, so you have to learn to trust God and hand the people you love over to his care."

I now trust God with the emptiness left by my lack of a normal family experience. He fills the space with healthy relationships, time with my children, and my grandkids. I no longer have to fill the space with hurtful people or memories. One of my favorite quotes is, "Friends become our chosen family." I have found this saying to be so true in my life.

I still have painful moments. It is okay to grieve the loss of something you wanted so badly. But if we stay stuck in the grief and pain, we will be crippled for the rest of our lives. We have to eventually move into acceptance in order to heal.

Generational Family Trap

Many of us stay lost and we waste a lot of time in our pain before opening the doors to all God has waiting for us. We blame our parents. *If only my life was different. If only I had a normal family, then I wouldn't have all these problems.* Or *if only they would've never done this or that.*

There is no doubt that every child deserves a loving childhood, but if we stay stuck in our pain and never uncover our issues, then the dysfunction will be passed down to our children.

Being stuck is the generational trap. My parents grew up in broken homes and never dealt with their issues. Then they got married and had six children that they raised while filled with pain from their past. Their pain caused a lot of unnecessary abuse, and neglect.

As a child I was starving for love, affection, and attention, and this affected me as an adult woman, but today I no longer need the approval or attention of others to survive. I have learned how to renew my mind in God's Word, understanding He created me in His image and loves me just the way I am—flaws and all. To help take away my fear and abandonment issues of not having the parents I desired, I've held on to this scripture: "Even if my father and mother abandon me, the Lord will hold me close" (Psalm 27:10 NLT).

In my mid-twenties I started to recognize the continued role I was playing in the dysfunctional family. I was repeating history. The father of my three children had a lot of character traits like my father, and I became addicted to him and our relationship. I desperately wanted to try to change him and make it work. I couldn't take being abandoned by one more person, and I didn't want my children to grow up without their father. What I was really trying to do was relive my childhood experience through this relationship, but I was determined to do it differently. Deep down inside I didn't want to fail. I wanted that family I'd always wanted. But the problems were huge. When we first met, he was thirteen, and I was fourteen. We got pregnant with our first child when he was fourteen, and I was fifteen. We were both clueless teenagers, and to top it off, we both grew up in broken homes. I can see now that there was no way I was going to get what I was searching for in that relationship.

We can put a lot of false and unrealistic expectations on the other person in our relationships.

Maybe this is where you find yourself today in a relationship desperately searching for love, but I have learned you must first love yourself before you can receive love.

Unfortunately, I have watched my children suffer with similar problems. I want to help them or take their pain, but I know this is their journey, and I need to give them the dignity to figure their life out just like I had to.

I've witnessed history repeat itself. I fell into a pattern of repeating what I experienced growing up. Even though this wasn't the goal I set for myself, the pattern just happened, and when it did, I didn't know what I had fell into was the generational trap.

God's grace and unconditional love can take our mess and turn it into a beautiful message if we let Him. I can pray for every generational curse to be broken off of my children, my grandchildren, and me. Until someone is willing to stand up and say, *no more* and stop the pattern, the sins will continue to run through the family line. My children in the beginning of their young lives were being brought up in a broken home environment.

Looking back now it was just one big puddle of brokenness, and we were all swimming in it trying to do the best that we could at the time and even now they don't see their dad because he struggles with addiction and pain from his childhood.

When my eyes opened to this truth, I was motivated to examine my life a little deeper. What can I do to break this cycle? How can I get healthier so I can support my children and live by example?

The first thing I needed was to control what I allowed into my environment as much as I could. I started protecting what my children were exposed to. I didn't become a control freak, even though it probably looked that way to others. But when you are brought up in addiction and dysfunction there are usually other family members who think it's normal. So when your kids are invited over to play and you say *no*, they are not going to like your answer.

Addiction has run rampant in my family and it has left me with much heartache and devastation. Addicts tend to take their loved one on an emotional roller coaster ride until someone jumps off and takes a stand.

Sometimes I feel guilt when I see my children suffering. I am careful not to beat myself up, but I am reminded once again the pain addiction can cause.

It doesn't matter how many years have gone by or how many years I've been working on my healing and recovery, the pain still runs deep in my heart. I am reminded almost daily how this disease has affected my whole family: siblings, cousins, nieces and nephews, aunts, and uncles. If I could run away from the effects addiction has had on my life and family, I would. But unfortunately I can't. This is my life, and I've learned I didn't cause it, and *I can't control* what other people's choices are. My upbringing and life experiences are something I can't escape, so why not use them for good?

If we want to live productive lives, it's important to work through our losses, so we can come to grips with accepting what our lives really are and aren't. If we don't take these steps each and every day, we could easily fall back into self-destructive numbing behaviors. For some reason God chose me to be born, and He chose you. He also picked our parents and our families of origin. Our job is to find strength in walking out this life He gave us. And I encourage you to find that strength.

So what are we to do if we find ourselves a victim of our circumstances?

We simply work on getting help by taking the necessary steps to heal and walk in freedom. But in order to start this process, you have to recognize the patterns that are holding you back and affecting your life today.

First, don't try to deal with all your pain at once. If you're struggling with an addiction, start there. Find a recovery program, change your environment, then find someone safe to help you start working through all your pain.

You can be free. If I can get free from all my addictions, patterns, and negative thinking, so can you!

reflection

Take a deep breath for a moment. I've given you a lot to think about in this chapter. Right now you may be thinking *it's too overwhelming*, or *it's too late for me*, or *gosh, I messed up my kids*. All this is just negative thinking that wants keep you in bondage … release these thoughts to God every time they come.

It's not for us to fix our life or anybody else's life. We present our needs and requests before God and then we wait for His direction. Let's talk about some practical steps and prayers we can lay before God. Through prayer and spiritual growth, we can more easily put our past behind us and move forward to achieve all that God has planned for us.

1. Examine your life. Are you still struggling with any patterns that are keeping you stuck? What about negative thoughts? Do you pretend to be okay when you're not? Do you put on a front by showing up in the world all put together in your appearance when you are dying inside? Ask God to help you be your true self and ask Him to help you let go of anything that interferes with your healing.

2. Is there someone you need to forgive? Ask God to show you if there is anybody. Do you find yourself saying they don't deserve to be forgiven? Unforgiveness will only keep you held in the patterns you are trying to get free from. Believe it or not, when we don't forgive, we suffer more than the abuser.

3. Have you ever had thoughts like these? *There is no hope for me. I'll be like this forever. I feel so alone. No one else has these problems.* Write these thoughts out on paper, so they get out of your head. Now look at your list. These words are not truth. Ask God to show you His plan for your life. God can and will heal us of anything if we let Him in, especially when we let go of areas we are trying to control.

prayer

Dear God,

I'm ready to release the wounds of my childhood. Please help me understand that what I experienced growing up was not my fault. Even though I wasn't in control of my upbringing, I am in control of my future. Heal me of the confusion that comes from being raised in addiction. Help me sort through my past so I can be a healthy individual. You are my strength, my healer, and my comforter. In Jesus' name I pray. Amen.

scripture

"And he said to her, 'Daughter, your faith has made you well. Go in peace. Your suffering is over'" (Mark 5:34 NLT).

"But if you refuse to forgive others, your Father will not forgive your sins" (Matthew 6:15 NLT).

"But if we confess our sins to him, he is faithful and just to forgive us our sins and to cleanse us from all wickedness" (1 John 1:9 NLT).

CHAPTER 6

Trusting the recovery process

Starting the healing process requires a willingness to look at our past with an open heart, asking God what happened to us. Only then can we face our pain, fear, and abandonment issues and break free of the lies that our wounds tell us. This openness may mean admitting that our parents or caregivers were unable to provide for us emotionally, physically, financially, or spiritually.

The key to recovery is inviting God into our brokenness. The way our brains protect us is by not allowing us to put the full picture together when we've experienced trauma. But this protection can lead us to second-guessing ourselves as to whether the event actually happened. I often felt as if something was wrong but I didn't know what. I was filled with fear and anxiety, but I couldn't put my finger on what was causing it. I now know that I had suppressed a lot of memories in order to survive all that I had been through—and was still going through.

As I walked through my recovery, I learned that the healing process is the hardest journey for trauma survivors. It takes a lot of courage and strength to walk through and trust the process. The healing journey can sometimes feel like one step forward and ten steps backward. There were many days when I felt like I would never heal.

A friend once said, "You didn't get here overnight, so don't be so hard on yourself or expect a quick fix. Give yourself time to heal."

I needed a deep emotional healing, and once I started this process, my identity needed to be restored—and my thought process. I worked daily on renewing my mindset with God's truth and allowing safe people like my husband, spiritual mom, and mentor to speak into my life. These things combined reminded me of my true identity and that I was worthy of love. There were many days when I wanted to give up and felt like the healing processes wasn't working.

You might be thinking right now, *I don't have a support system.* I believe God will bring you the right people. I've seen God work in so many people's lives that I am confident He will do it for you. Jesus said, "You can ask for anything in my name, and I will do it, so that the Son can bring glory to the Father" (John 14:13 NLT). I believe that God loves to heal our hearts so we can give Him all the glory.

In this chapter I will share part of my journey to inspire you to trust in your process. I will touch on some of my emotional healing, and what it took to restore my identity and renew my mind with God's truth and positive affirmations. Every part of the process began restoring me back to the person God created me to be in the first place.

Was healing an easy journey? Absolutely not. Did I want to give up sometimes? Yes. But I am so glad I didn't and was able to follow through. I would not be here today writing this chapter had I given up on the process. The healing journey has benefited my life for the better, including my physical health, relationships, and finances. It was exhausting to be tormented by negative voices, self-hate, self-doubt, and destructive patterns.

I often hear people say they don't have time to go to counseling. This is a sad situation as it keeps the past buried. But if you are reading this, I am hopeful that my story will prompt you to do the hard work so you can live a life of happiness and freedom, no matter what your past experience may be.

There are recovery groups addressing many topics today. There are counseling offices that offer counseling sessions on a sliding scale for people who don't have health insurance, and there are churches that offer free counseling. So whatever your situation, I encourage you to not wait. When my personal life was broken, so was everything else.

What can you do to start? Start with what's in front of you. Maybe it's making a list of some small action steps you can take to get the help you need. If you are not sure, reach out to someone you can trust like a pastor, close friend, or mentor.

When I was twenty-four years old, I was invited to a recovery program. My kids were little—around the ages of seven, four, and one. Even though I was a young mom and could have been out with my friends partying at the bars, I chose to find a babysitter to go to an hour recovery meeting instead, because I was desperate to get help. In time these meetings paid off for me, opening doors to help me understand that I was severely affected from growing up in alcoholism, drug abuse and violence. As months passed by, then years, I gained strength and wisdom from other people in the program, and I began making healthier choices in my life and learning how to put up clear boundaries to take care of myself.

If we don't confront the damage that the abuse and neglect caused, it will continue to do damage to us. I have witnessed people in their sixties and seventies still dealing with wounds caused by other people.

I understand that it is easier to ignore or gloss over your pain. We are all on different journeys, but if you allow God to shine a light on all the garbage you may have buried in your heart, recovery and restoration can begin.

When God helps us put our story together, life makes more sense. We find peace, and we can start to help other people by sharing our story of hope and recovery.

Emotional Healing

If you want to be free, you must take the necessary steps toward making yourself whole. What most people don't realize is that it's okay to admit that your parents or caregivers were flawed human beings. There's this wise saying I think of when I think of my parents, "a man without arms can't hug." My parents weren't capable of loving me with unconditional love but that doesn't mean I should deny the fact that their behavior was unacceptable. You are not betraying your parents or caregivers by speaking the truth of how it affected your life.

Also, as you walk through the process of facing your pain, be patient with yourself, as some of your weaknesses or coping mechanisms may surface. These are the habits we picked up along the way to help us survive. I had many, and to this day they still surface. When my mind gets in a really dark place or I find myself isolating, I know it's time to pick up the phone and call a friend and get out of the house. Now that

I can recognize these habits, I ask God to help me instead of beating myself up.

It takes a lot of courage to do this work. As you continue this journey, be gentle with yourself as memories and feelings arise. Give yourself time to grieve the losses that have been buried. And remember this journey is not to be traveled alone.

I strongly want to encourage you to ask Jesus to come into your life and help you on this new path you are about to take. For many years I tried so many other alternatives to try to take my pain away and what I learned in all of this was Jesus is the only one who can heal us, and He is the only one who will rescue us from pain of our past.

I spent way too long inviting other things into my life to take away my pain, and it never worked. Things like an eating disorder, cutting, drugs, alcohol, sex, shopping, perfectionism ... I can go on and on.

If you are to the point where you feel like you've tried it all and you are hurting, take that step of faith that I did. Ask Jesus if He is real? Tell Him you want to know Him more. He cares about you. All of you. Your fears, your thought process, self-doubt, and all the emotional pain you may be carrying.

My abandonment and rejection were deep. My parents who raised me didn't love themselves, and they didn't know how to love me properly. When you have someone you want to love you so badly, especially parents, and they don't know how, it hurts. The sting of rejection is real. The result was self-hate, and I didn't understand why I hated myself until I honestly examined my childhood and began the process of forgiveness for all the rejection and abuse. For instance, when I would come home with my mom we would walk into a beer flying across the room barely missing our heads because my father was in one of his drinking rages. This left me so confused trying to figure out what was wrong with me that he would want to do this to me. It always felt that the abuse towards me was my fault.

When I started my healing journey I wanted to understand the background my parents came from and it turned out they came from a lot of dysfunction and addiction.

My father was an orphan most of his life. His father had been an alcoholic who abused him and his brothers. From a young age, my father lived on the streets, and he learned how to survive by being street smart.

He fed himself by stealing food and eating out of the trash as early as the age eight years old, and he learned how to defend himself through fighting. These behaviors rolled right into his parenting skills. As I look back now, my father didn't discipline us like a father should. It was more like we were one of his friends, and if he didn't like the way we responded to him or the way we looked at him, it usually meant him getting violent with us like we were somebody on the streets. It wasn't out of the ordinary for him to chase one of us down. At his funeral, people who knew him said, "Nobody wanted to mess with your dad." He was known as being crazy and nobody wanted to cross him. Growing up when my dad would blow up that meant somebody usually got hurt.

In 2006 I worked as a bailiff in the small town that I grew up in. The Judge that I worked for noticed my last name and asked me if I was related to and then he proceeded to say my father's name. Nervously, I said yes, that is my dad. He said, "oh my, I use to serve search warrants to your house all the time. I wasn't sure how to respond so I quickly walked away."

Some of my father's behavior's carried over into my parenting. Giving my life to Jesus and my recovery has helped me to learn how to break free from those patterns of behaviors.

Starting in middle school, I became an aggressive teenager, and I was kicked out of school for fighting. My behaviors were a lot like my father's, full of aggression, stealing, and using drugs and alcohol. When I became a teen mom at age fifteen and again at eighteen, my emotions were out of control, and I didn't know how to parent my children.

I started my recovery program in my early twenties, and a woman who was trying to help me heard me screaming at my daughter. She called me out. I am very grateful for that experience. I may not have liked it at the time, because I am sure I felt a lot of shame. What I learned from this situation was that I didn't need to parent my children with fear to make them listen to me. She instructed me that I didn't need to scream in rage or use profanity to get my children's attention. She explained "the angrier you get, I want you to actually practice whispering, and get on their eye level." She said, "I want you to mean what you say and be firm but you don't have to instill fear in them."

This experience was another important part of my healing journey, learning new behaviors and undoing the old ones.

My father's aggression and alcoholism were passed on to him. And it was passed on to me. This continued pattern is called a generational curse. Understanding the passing down of these behaviors may help you understand some of the battles you find yourself in today.

I was in a spiritual battle for a very long time. I was locked up by suppressed memories; abandonment, and rejection issues were controlling my life.

I had so many issues and pent-up emotions that I had no clue what to do with them. At the time, I had no idea about the root cause. But I knew something was terribly wrong with my home life and me.

By the age of thirteen, I had turned to drugs and alcohol, smoking rock cocaine with a neighbor, being sexually active, and getting in fights in school. I was out of control and very angry. I am not proud of my behavior, but I am sharing this to show you how the generational pattern will repeat itself whether we welcome it or not. I had no plan for my life, and I never wrote anger and rebellion as my goals. Life just happened. To be honest, I didn't think about how to act. It was the life I was exposed to growing up and I lived it. I was acting out because of what I saw and what I experienced. My choices were my coping mechanisms.

My Breaking Point

In my early thirties, I went through my second divorce, and life was hard. This was a very scary time for me, especially since I was an adult woman who was very good at pretending I had it all together. It was time for me to let go and surrender my life and all my control to God. I didn't follow Him right away—it was a back and forth process that God took me through. He was getting me to a place where I could trust him at a deeper level. Many days I cried out to God. *What will people think of me if they know about my life, my history, who my family is, or where I came from? I grew up on welfare, my dad was in prison most of my life. My mom was never home because she struggled with her own addictions. I was in a gang. How embarrassing,* I thought. I was full of shame, and I was full of secrets. I didn't want anyone to know the real me, yet I could no longer hide my pain. The affects of addiction were wreaking havoc on my life, my entire family—including my children.

God began teaching me that I wasn't in control of what happened to me as a child or who my parents were. But I was in control of how to live the rest of my life. I wasn't in control of other people's behaviors (even though I wanted to be) but what I was in control of was how I would respond to what happened to me.

God gives us a choice whether or not we want to heal from our past. I believe God doesn't force us to do anything, but instead He gives us the option to walk into His freedom and forgiveness.

I had to let go of the fear of caring what people thought about me, and I needed to find someone I felt safe with so I could get help. I needed to be able to be honest with someone about my childhood.

I'll never forget when I started trauma therapy. My therapist's first response was, "I don't think I've ever met somebody with your level of trauma."

I was surprised. *Really?* What happened to me felt ordinary because it was all I knew. She helped me understand what was normal and what wasn't, because in order for me to start feeling better I had to identify my trauma.

To think that getting pregnant at fifteen and initiated into a gang was no big deal is pretty sad. When I was eleven years old, my dad got shot by a cop, and he was on the news, and there was a book written about what had happened to my family. But I thought that was ordinary.

My therapist helped me walk through all my traumatic memories. Maybe I shouldn't say all ... because I think God gave me just enough memories to heal my soul. When I got strong enough to revisit those dark places, I began to feel lighter, and the world started to look different. Every time I walked through one of those experiences, I felt Jesus comforting me and giving me the strength I needed.

I started to find strength in my pain. Instead of being a scared little girl, I turned into a warrior, thinking *wow, I did it*. I overcame a lot. I am still walking through some issues, and I believe these memories will be a part of my life until I get to heaven, but I know I don't have to walk this journey alone. I am surrounded by healthy people who love me, and I can feel the love of God.

When I was broken I was desperately searching for a place of acceptance and someone who would understand what I had been through, and God did that for me. He brought the right people. He helped me put a voice to all the pain I carried. He helped me make all the necessary changes I needed to make in my life.

I got to a point where I was willing to go to any measure for my healing. And if that meant driving my butt to trauma therapy every week and a recovery meeting, I was there.

All the trauma caught up to me. I could no longer hide behind my secrets. I could no longer suppress the pain. It was starting to seep out of my pores.

I needed professional help from a therapist who understood, but I also had spiritually mature people around me to help me understand I was also dealing with a lot of my parents' junk that was passed down to me.

Just like you pass the torch to the next runner, my parents handed me their stuff.

My discoveries helped me learn to pray in a different way. I asked God to show me where I needed to ask Him for forgiveness, especially for my own behaviors. I asked God to guide me and show me what I needed to do in order to get healed and whole.

I want to give you an example of a memory God gave me.

As a young girl, I was confused when I saw how a friend's house was clean and in order—full of decorations on the wall. There was even bathroom décor and clean towels. Sometimes I sat in their bathroom because it felt so peaceful, clean, and safe. I would just sit there and allow my feet to sink deep into the carpet. Of course, I didn't want to stay in there too long, because I didn't want someone to come knocking on the door to check on me.

Our home was under construction for a very long time. One of my brothers did most of the work while my dad was in prison. He was trying to remodel our bathroom. I remember there being a large piece of drywall hanging in the bathroom, but it didn't stay up for long because one day when I was fighting with my brother my body went flying through it.

There was something inside me that was attracted to the peace I felt in my friend's home. But when you are traumatized as a child, it's hard to understand what you are feeling. Looking back now I can see clearly. I loved the fact that her house had her parents at home, the house was clean, and they had food. I desired these things but didn't know how to express my needs at the time.

We didn't decorate our house; it was actually dirty all the time. Our home was usually full of holes in the wall from all the fighting that took place between us six children.

At my friend's home, one or both parents would be there. My dad had been in prison for a few years, and it felt like my mom was working all the time. Sometimes, I would get invited to stay for dinner, which would make me nervous and excited at the same time. What would it feel like to sit around a table with a family and eat with them? I remember one incident clearly.

As I sat at the table I remember feeling dirty, like I didn't belong. I knew deep down inside my family was very different from theirs. I was thinking, *what if this family knew where I came from?* My house was pretty much always dirty unless I cleaned it, but it didn't stay clean for too long, because so many people came in and out of our home. I remember sitting there at the table so afraid that they might find out who I really was. A girl whose father is in prison, who didn't have family dinners like this. What would they do if they knew? Would their daughter still be able to hang around me?

I clenched my fist as it rested on my lap, hoping they wouldn't ask me any questions that I would not know how to answer. You know like the usual ones. What sports do you play? Where do your parents work? What time do you have to be home?

Most of the time there were no house rules unless one of my brothers was trying to get me to listen to him. I hung out in the park until it was super late.

When these questions would come up, I felt like I wanted to take off running. Instead, I just sat there quietly, nervously squeezing my knees together.

I lived my childhood, hiding, feeling out of control, scared someone would know who I really was. My body was constantly tensed, and this led to many health problems that started in my childhood. If you are struggling with migraines or digestive issues, it could be from all the emotions still stuffed inside you.

Most people who grew up in addiction or have been abused in some way faced these same anxieties.

My healing has helped me let go of the shame of my past. I am no longer embarrassed of my life experience or what happened to me. Instead of looking at myself as a failure, I've started seeing myself as a survivor.

One of the worst feelings in the world is to hate yourself or to be ashamed of who you are. When I started being restored to my true self, it wasn't always easy, because I changed a lot. But I changed for the better. I lost people because most people I was hanging around with when I was broken were attracted to the weak parts of me. When I became stronger, some people did not know how to respond to the new me.

Identity and Renewing My Mind

After my emotional healing process, God started to restore my identity. And I had to walk by faith by believing what God's word said about me.

I used to look in the mirror and hate every part of me. I cut my arms and legs. I punched myself in the face and told myself horrible things. I went on my first diet when I was eighteen in hopes of losing enough weight to get some attention. I didn't understand why nobody loved me, and I felt abandoned. The pain was so deep that I didn't know how to explain it to anybody. I just felt like I wanted to die all the time.

But once God started healing those wounds, I was to able to get centered and start seeing myself the way He created me. I really don't believe I would have been able to change the way I saw myself until God revealed my brokenness.

I read positive affirmation cards. Some have Bible verses on them and some have positive quotes. I believe practicing this every day has helped me drown out the negative voices I used to hear in my head, which I believe were from my abusers.

Your recovery will take work. You can't just sit back and expect to feel better or change. You must take action steps to experience freedom.

If you don't seek God for your healing, you will spend your entire life giving your power to someone else because you weren't willing to go through the healing process of forgiving them and yourself.

What will you choose today?

reflection

When we hit a breaking point, we are ready to ask for help. We present our needs and requests to God the best that we know how, and then we wait for His direction.

As you learn about God's word, you will find that if we are faithful to Him and confess our weaknesses we will be forgiven. He is there ready to help. Through prayer and God promises, we will be ready to put our past behind us and move forward to achieve the great things He has planned for us.

1. Do you feel it's time to seek professional help? Spend some time praying about it. What is God telling you?

2. Take some time to examine your life by answering these questions: Are you still struggling with any patterns that are keeping you stuck? What about negative thoughts? Do you pretend to be okay when you're not? Do you put on a front by showing up in the world all put together through your appearance when you are dying inside?

3. Ask God to help you be your true self and ask Him to help you let go. If you answered yes to any of the questions above, prayerfully consider seeking help.

prayer

Dear God,
Please give me the strength to do the hard work of forgiving myself and anybody else I need to forgive, so I can live a life free of shame and guilt. You know my thoughts and patterns that I have used in order to survive the family dysfunction. Help me stay the course of my healing journey, even on the days when it feels like nothing is working. Always remind me to be gentle with myself and help me understand that healing is a process. I'm ready to surrender.
In Jesus' name I pray. Amen.

scripture

"Come to me, all you who are weary and burdened, and I will give you rest. Take my yoke upon you and learn from me, for I am gentle and humble in heart, and you will find rest for your souls. For my yoke is easy and my burden is light" (Matthew 11:28-30 NLT).

CHAPTER 7

Why I Left

Sometimes it might take complete separation from everything you've ever known in order to heal and find freedom. The more you heal, the more your true identity comes forth, and you no longer have to hide behind addictions or coping mechanisms.

Some people may never understand why I decided to pack up my house and children and move 1,800 miles away from everything I was used to and where I had lived for twenty years. Moving wasn't an easy decision for me. At times I felt like a scared little girl on the inside, but for a long time I had known this was something I needed to do.

When I made the decision to leave Las Vegas, everything seemed so perfect in my life. My husband and I had bought our first home; we had been married just a few years; I had a good job; we were both driving nice vehicles; and our kids were in sports. Seems like the family dream that everyone wants. And to top it off, I was in a popular weight-loss program and had hit my goal. On the outside all appeared as if I had it all together.

Yet nobody had a clue about all the energy it took to pretend we were the happy family.

Looking back now, I can understand why people leave for six months to eighteen months to go to a treatment facility, leaving their current surroundings. To heal and find out who they really are they need time away from the stress of life and all the family turmoil and addictions. This was the scenario I was in, but I couldn't recognize it until I got out and had some time away.

As I would put distance between the family dysfunction and myself, the less it felt normal when I would go back around it.

When I left Las Vegas in 2004, we lived in a nice neighborhood, my boys were playing football, and my daughter was in cheerleading. I loved my job working at the Juvenile Court school with at-risk children and working part-time taking care of abused and neglected children.

It had felt like my life was flourishing, yet at the same time it felt like the weight of the world was dragging me down.

I was tired and my body was so exhausted from hiding all my secrets.

I spent many nights lying awake, crying myself to sleep with fear and anxiety because my then-husband (now ex) who was an alcoholic wouldn't come home most nights. I used to be concerned if he was going to lose his job, so I would call in work for him and make up all kinds of excuses, because I knew we needed to pay our bills and we had kids to feed. Fear constantly gripped me and kept me in full-blown anxiety.

Repeating the Past

I was afraid, wondering who would come to our door next. There were people knocking at our door in all hours of the night, or my husband was banging on the door drunk after a night of partying in the bars. I was always afraid because the type of people he chose to hang around with were the type of people I used to hang around with before I gave my life to Christ. And I knew their mentality. I don't say this in a judgmental way, but once I surrendered my life to Jesus, my eyes became opened to the situations I used to put myself in. I knew I needed a new set of friends fast to protect myself and my children.

My house was shot up by gang members while my one-year-old son was inside sleeping in his crib. My home was robbed twice. My dad had been shot by the police, and my husband's mom was shot seven times and murdered. These events are just a handful of the things I experienced while growing up in Las Vegas. I used to put myself in dangerous places because I had no knowledge of healthy fear. Being initiated into a gang at an early age and growing up in that environment, I had no fear of death or pain, especially after all that I had witnessed.

But when I started to change my life for the better—or I should say when God opened my eyes—I was no longer comfortable around the same people or in the same places I use to hang out.

Instead of being comfortable I started to avoid them because I was fearful. I knew I needed to not only get myself out of this environment, but also my three children.

Constant fear and longing for the life I knew God had waiting for me motivated me to make the move.

It seemed as if my life was starting to parallel some of my upbringing, even though I made a strong vow to myself that I would never be like my parents or live that way. But when my family left the small farm in Indiana and moved to Las Vegas, I was exposed to a lot. If someone had not shared the message of hope with me about Jesus dying on the cross for my sins and explained that He had a better life for me, I don't think I would be alive today or free of drugs and alcohol. But the gospel helped me start to seek a better life and get out.

As a new believer in Christ, I was learning to pray, and I watched different pastors on TV. One pastor caught my attention. Pastor Charles Stanley was an older man, and when he spoke it felt as if his voice had filled the atmosphere of my home. His voice was so serene and peaceful. I heard him say what God expected of us as a family, as parents, and as spouses. It was definitely something I wasn't used to, but I always desired it. God allowed me to meet Pastor Stanley after I moved to West Michigan about sixteen years later at a book signing, and I got to thank him for getting me through some tough times in my life.

As far back as I can remember—like around age five and six—I would play alone and dream about living a peaceful life. I wondered what life would be like without screaming or fighting or my dad being so mean and violent, or my mom not leaving me. To be able to call on these memories that I had at a young age is very important to me now, because remembering them helps me realize that peace and quiet is something I have always craved. To this day, it is very important for me to have calm in my life so my trauma doesn't get triggered. Too much excitement or noise can still make me anxious.

Even though I was being controlled by my life circumstances, I knew someday I was going to find peace, and I did.

Children who have been deeply traumatized in their childhoods either make promises to themselves that they won't repeat what happened to them, or they repeat some of the exact behaviors they swore they would never do.

It's interesting now to see how my siblings and I are different in many ways—especially the way we respond to life circumstances. I'm not saying that one way is right or wrong, but it's interesting to see how our upbringing has affected us all differently. It seems like my siblings and I have a different perspective of what happened in our childhood, because we were all fragmented in different ways. Some chose to party with my dad up until the day he passed away, I kept my distance at times because the pain of old memories was so great for me personally. It's so important to know that it's okay to do whatever you need to do to heal from your childhood or past abuse. Understanding the different ways to heal took a long time for me to comprehend, and it took a lot of people like my mentor and therapist to remind me.

As a young mom, I realized how my behavior mirrored my parents' behavior, it really scared me, and the sad part was it would just show up without me even giving any thought to it.

Let me give you an example of what I am talking about. One night I threw my teenage daughter up against the wall and started calling her all kinds of dirty names. My veins were popping out of my forehead as I was screaming at the top of my lungs saying curse words that my dad used to call me. It felt as if something had snapped inside of me. I'm not proud of this night. I felt a lot of shame the next day, but after praying I realized that behavior was exactly what my dad used to do to me. During the next few days, I asked God for forgiveness and asked Him to please help me if this rage tried to re-surface. There was a lot of anger trapped inside me that I was not yet aware of. In my prayer time with God, I asked him to examine my heart and show me what's in there. To this day I own about seventy journals I have written in my secret place for the last twenty years.

When I felt God was nudging me to write this book so I could help other people like myself who have been traumatized or affected by addiction, I told him *I can't, I'm not a writer*, next thing you know I heard a voice in my heart whisper, *really, then what's all this?* as I stared at all my journals on a bookshelf.

Leaving Physically

So why did I move? I hope by now I have made my reasons pretty clear. I'm not saying that everyone must also move across the country, but I needed to get away. Mentally and physically I needed a break from all the stress and not only the current stress but all the trauma that was trapped inside my body from my childhood and all I had experienced after my family moved to Las Vegas.

The drive inside of me that wanted to change made the transition easier in the beginning. I knew if I wanted a better life, then it was going to take a change of atmosphere and space.

Please don't pick up and move because I did. Instead prayerfully consider your situation and circumstances. I just know that I needed a fresh start in order to find myself.

Leaving Emotionally

Did you know we are not in control of someone else's life? But we are in control of how we want to live the rest of our lives. One thing I knew for sure is that I wanted to live a happy life, and I was going to do whatever it took to protect my children from violence, drugs, and alcohol.

In this life I know it's not possible to have perfect peace all the time or a life free of chaos, but I do believe we can remove unnecessary drama and pain once we identify its source.

Let me explain what I mean and what brought me to the point of feeling like I needed to make the move and leave my familiar surroundings. The details are not easy for me to share, but I feel they are necessary steps some people need to take in order to heal.

After I made the move, I questioned myself many times about whether I did the right thing. People would say, *you think you are better than us*, etc … But the stronger I got and the more I healed, the clearer I saw their words for what they really were.

The Bible makes it very clear about the issues of the heart. It addresses the broken heart, it tells us to ask God to examine our hearts, and it warns us to guard our hearts because our hearts determine the courses of our lives. You can read some scriptures on this at the end of this chapter.

Before I made the move I had a broken heart that was leading me down a very destructive path.

I would like to ask you a few questions … Why do people drink alcohol even when they are in liver failure? Why do people cut their bodies even though they are beautiful? Why do so many women starve themselves because they feel fat, but they are withering away? Why are people secretly addicted to pornography but embarrassed to get help?

For a long time I did not know why people wouldn't stop or get help. These are all self-destructive behaviors, and every person who struggles with these behaviors or addictions is ashamed of them. They feel embarrassed that they can't stop.

I know this feeling oh so well—this is how I felt for a very long time. The more I was self-destructing the deeper I would go into isolation. But what was causing me to act out in ways I did not want to? I didn't know, and I was so confused and embarrassed that I was caught in these addictions. And I couldn't ask my family for help, because they were struggling with some of the exact behaviors.

Heart Issues. Yes, I believe these problems are issues of the heart. Let's say it together one more time; issues of the heart are what cause people to act out. If people are struggling or acting out, they have some kind of heart issue or wound in their heart. When we have been wounded, or we have wounded someone else because of generational sin, it becomes a heart issue. We feel guilty without even knowing it. We start to self-sabotage more and more. Then here comes the enemy or your own guilt whispering in your ear, *you see, you will never change. You are just like your parents. Look at you; you binged again; look how fat you are.* This repeats the vicious cycle of the behavior all over again until we know how to stop it.

For me it took moving away and breaking free. Moving was the beginning of a long process, and at times it was a very confusing progression for me. Today, I know it was necessary. In order for me to see what was wounding my heart, I had to be distant from it for a season. As I grew stronger, got more inner healing, and learned who God created me to be, I got a clearer vision of what I wanted out of life, and it has helped me to walk into His plan for me, which is to encourage others through my story of healing. For me to be able to do this though, I had to guard myself from people, places, and actions that were still wounding my heart and triggering my trauma.

This newfound freedom came with a price I had to pay. It meant giving up everything I was familiar with in life. Including abuse, addiction, codependent relationships, constant chaos, and the need to know all the family business.

Remember it is not being judgmental to stay away from people and activities that are hurting you and are toxic for your life. Staying away is how you protect yourself from further damage. The day you put up healthy boundaries and make some changes to better your life, you will hear comments like, *you've changed, you are no longer fun to be around.* People will even say, *you make me feel bad about myself* or *you think you are holier than thou.* These are all the words I heard when I stopped being involved in unnecessary drama, even if it was family or my adult children.

It's You or Them

It did not make a difference how much time I spent trying to keep my family put together or begging my husband at the time to change or keep his job. There was much more.

I had promised myself I would never marry an alcoholic like my dad. But I did and repeated some of the same patterns I witnessed growing up in addiction.

How could this be happening to me? I thought. *I have worked so hard to try to do things the right way.*

One of my favorite statements is, "You can't have behavior change on the outside until you deal with the issues of the inside." People will try to make changes to their lives, but the modifications are only temporary because they didn't allow God to heal their hearts.

Back-and-Forth Process

There were times I didn't recognize myself. I discovered much about myself, like what I enjoyed and who and what I didn't care to be around.

For many years, I placed temporary Band-Aids on some deep wounds that needed a lot more attention. These brief fixes helped me survive for a while, but never helped me grow into the person I wanted to become. To be my authentic self, I needed to be healed of past abuse. When I did the work to heal, it felt like I was seeing my life with a new set of eyes. I felt like I was in a coma for a very long time, because I wasn't living my life or enjoying it.

Physically, emotionally, and spiritually I needed a breakthrough, and I wanted away from everything: the noise, the addiction, family fighting, lying, cheating, stealing, and gossiping about one another.

But even though I knew I needed to leave, I was sometimes confused because I missed the people and strangely, I missed the drama too. I wanted to spend time with the people, but every time I came back from a visit I struggled with my eating disorder and self-hate. During this season, I worked closely with my therapist, spiritual mom, and mentor, and they all kept reminding me of my new goals in different ways.

None of these people who helped me wanted to tell me what to do, because they wanted me to see truth for myself. If I wanted to heal, I needed to stay away from the places and people that caused me to feel bad about myself. It wasn't that anyone was trying to intentionally hurt me, but the words they said or certain behaviors would trigger my pain from past wounds from childhood. When I would hear about the abuse in my family, who was struggling with an addiction, who was in jail, condescending remarks said about me by so and so, or how certain people didn't agree with the way I choose to live my life, I would walk away feeling bad about myself. All this stole my peace and joy.

The pattern I found myself in for many years was that I would start to feel better physically and mentally, and my self-confidence started to improve. My relationship with God was becoming stronger, and I was learning that my identity was in Him, not my upbringing or things that happened to me in the past.

All it took was one visit or contact with certain people from my past, and suddenly those good feelings were gone. It felt like I had been sucked in a vacuum and brought back right where I had started from.

I continued in this back-and-forth process until I got strong enough to say, "No more." I needed to become stronger in this new foundation for a while before I allowed myself to go back into any environment that would destroy all the hard work I had done.

One of the hardest steps I've ever taken in life is to put up boundaries with those who were the closest to me, including family and good friends. I never wanted to disappoint anybody as a kid, and I sure didn't want to as an adult. When you grow up in abuse and neglect, you are starving for love and attention, so to have anybody mad at you can feel terrifying.

When you create boundaries people will be upset with you. That's because they are used to the old you, and when you restrict contact, people become uncomfortable or they won't like the fact that you are no longer a pushover. People were actually shocked when I told them *no* and that I didn't want to do or be involved in their activities.

Limiting and sometimes losing these people I loved caused me to grieve during this season, but the new people God put in my life to support me helped me keep moving forward and reminded me that I was doing the right thing.

If nothing was to change in my life, I knew nothing was going to change with me.

Remember nothing is forever … draw close to God and let him heal you as you take whatever necessary steps you need to take in order to feel safe and protected. And do what you can to get the help and support you need. Surround yourself with healthy, mature people who can speak into your life until you feel confident in your new way of living.

Not only was I grieving the family that I really never had, I was also grieving everything that I was used to and all the stuff I had experienced growing up. When you walk away from dysfunctions, you will actually have withdrawals from the adrenalin rush you get from being in a constant state of crisis.

Many days I had mixed emotions that I didn't know what to do with or where these feelings were coming from. But I kept putting my trust in God, and I would say little prayers like, *God, I am going to trust you no matter what, even when things don't make sense to me, I will trust you to show me if there is anything else I need to do or change.*

The more I started to change, the more time and energy I had in my life. I started to experience what I thought I would never do, like enjoying planting flowers or decorating my house.

Some of the changes I made in my life were not easy at first and came with a lot of second-guessing myself. I was responding and acting in the opposite way I had in my entire life and sometimes the negative tapes would play in my head. So often, I had to remind myself, "This is my life and I am worth fighting for."

All these changes didn't happen overnight. As I grew and became stronger, the easier it was to stand in my truth and use my voice.

I was actually fulfilling a promise that I made to myself as a child, but I didn't realize it until I got a lot of recovery and distance under my belt.

When I started to recognize and work on my patterns, learning which ones were serving me purpose and which ones weren't, I was able to make major changes in my life.

As a little girl, when there was so much commotion going on in my home, I used to sit and dream and tell myself, someday I am going to run away from all of this and find a peaceful place to live. These were promises I made to myself, and they made a deep impression on my heart that was covered up by all the pain and fear.

I have never told anybody what I was thinking or really spoke about it much but as I sit here writing this chapter, I can see that all along I was fighting to get to the place I am today.

I never knew why I had those thoughts, but looking back now I can see why. In the last few years God has given me many dreams of me sitting in peaceful places, and from a distance I can see a lot of people hurting. To me these dreams speak, *you have done the hard work and you have found peace.* That doesn't mean I live a life free of pain, but I do now know how to take care of myself and protect my home to provide a safe place for me. My husband is very sensitive to this need in my life.

That part of me back then that always wanted to be free and get away one day … I can tell her now, "You are free!"

Never give up. It's not too late for you to make it out of whatever you are going through.

reflection

As you read through this chapter, I would like you to prayerfully consider how God is speaking to you and your situation. This chapter was never written to give people permission to just drop everything and everyone and walk away from your current responsibilities, but it is to encourage people that they deserve healing and freedom here on earth. Whatever your situation may be, my hope is that you find the strength to do what it takes to heal and live a calm, happy, and peaceful life.

1. What would your life look like if you had no fear, no debt, or any struggles from your past? I want you to take a minute and dream with me. Sometimes it's hard to believe we deserve a life free of hardship when that's all we've known, but you can have it. Take some time and write a description about the life you really want to live.

2. What would it look like for you to get rid of all your secrets and live in freedom? Write some steps you can take to get closer to this goal.

prayer

Dear God,
I'm asking you to open my eyes to your dreams for me. Make what stands in my way clear to me. I don't want to live a life stuck in trauma or pain from my past. I know you are capable of getting me to a place of complete healing, peace, and joy. Please help me go to those deep places I need in order to find the rest and healing I desire to walk out your perfect plan for me. In Jesus' name I pray. Amen.

scripture

"Guard your heart above all else, for it determines the course of your life" (Proverbs 4:23 NLT).

"Even those closest to you—your parents, brothers, relatives, and friends—will betray you. And some of you will be killed. And everyone will hate you because of your allegiance to me. But not a hair of your head will perish! By standing firm, you will win souls" (Luke 21:16–19 NLT).

"And everyone who has given up houses or brothers or sisters or father or mother or children or property, for my sake, will receive a hundred times as much in return and will have eternal life" (Matthew 19:29 NLT).

reclaiming our True identity

In order to find our true identity, we must begin the process of challenging the things we learned while growing up in abuse and addiction. I have learned that no abandonment is more painful than abandoning our true self.

Have you ever felt like you had no clue about who you are, and if you are seeking change, you don't even know where to begin? If you have ever felt this way, I want you to know I truly understand. Because I too was lost and confused for a long time, asking myself these same questions.

If you feel lost and confused, it is not uncommon.

The enemy of our soul comes to steal, kill, and destroy our identity through abuse and neglect. And this can take place in the home we grew up in. The longer the enemy can keep us wounded, the less effective we will be in this life.

Discovering our true identity may be a difficult process but not impossible. The healing process begins with the willingness to be open and look at our soul wounds. Remembering the experiences that nearly destroyed us usually starts with revisiting past abuse. Being hurt or rejected is one of the most painful situations to go through. Scripture is full of examples of family dysfunction. When reading the Bible you will see family members betraying, hurting, and rejecting each other. Sometimes family may be the primary source of our pain. This may be confusing at first to comprehend but until you understand this you will stay stuck and confused, wondering what you did wrong to cause these people to hurt you.

The more that you go back and look at what happened to you will allow you to see how your heart was assaulted by these behaviors. This gives God the opportunity to heal your heart which leads to wholeness. And once you become healed in your new identity, it's more than likely people, and your family members, are not going to like it. They are used to the old you who never spoke up for yourself and had no boundaries.

Friends who have been through similar woundedness themselves can more fully understand the impact we are going through. And there may be seasons in our life when friends can feel a lot closer than family. They understand how we feel, and they accept us in the good and bad times when we are going through the healing process. Most people who cause us pain are usually broken themselves, and they don't fully understand the love of God.

Growing up in a dysfunctional family can be stressful and chaotic. We are taught at a young age not to feel. We learn to stay on guard at all times, because we never know what might happen next. When something traumatic takes place in the home with one of our family members, we are taught to not talk, trust or feel about what is going on and the next day everybody pretended as if nothing ever happened.

In recovery, we call this pretense, denial.

There are so many examples I could share, but there is one that comes to my mind first. When I was around age seven in the first grade, we lived in a light blue house in Iowa. It had a small porch attached to the front. In our yard off to the side was a parked camper. One night in the winter my dad had some friends over, and they were drinking together. I always knew to stay out-of-sight if I could, because I never knew what was going to happen. As it got later and time for bed, I remember hearing their conversations getting louder and louder. Then the noise stopped for a few minutes, and I heard broken glass and screaming. At that moment my little mind started working overtime to block out everything until the noise was gone, and I could fall asleep.

The next day I had to go to school. I got up in the morning, had my cereal, and as usual everybody sat in silence. As I stepped out onto the porch on my way to school, I saw a trail of blood that led over to the camper and when the blood trail hit the snow it appeared as if there was a lot more. The memories of this event that are so vivid in my mind today—once the blood hit the snow it seemed a lot brighter than it did on the sidewalk. I remember looking at that blood and saying to myself, *oh, that must be from last night,* as I shrugged my shoulders never acknowledging the trauma that just took place the night before. Instead I ran off to the bus because I was so accustomed to not feeling my emotions.

There were many scenarios like this that I faced while growing up, but no one ever talked about them at home. Half the time I didn't know what was going on. I lived in a numb state. *Don't talk. Don't feel. Don't react.* These behaviors followed me into my adolescent years and into my adult life.

Imagine a child learning to be numb. How can anyone function like this? Let alone know who they really are? If we can't get in touch with how we feel, we will never be able to receive love or give love.

I later learned what happened that night. My dad and his so-called buddies got into a drunken brawl, and my dad got beat up very bad by some of the men who had a tie rod and hit him several times in the head with it. I still never heard the full details of the story, but just enough to validate that the memories I was having as an adult were true.

Not too long after this, I was left at the home of my aunt and uncle. My teenage cousin, who lived there, held me down on a bunk bed with my legs open while he was grinding his body on mine with force. Once again because my little mind was conditioned to not talk, and not feel, I thought this must be another thing I have to go through. Memories like this are hard to actually state as facts because I believe as trauma survivors we do such a good job blocking out horrific memories.

This is why I thought something was wrong with me, and I never understood what was normal in life. Because, I was a victim, yet I thought I was wrong. Healing comes when we, as victims, understand that most of our painful experiences were not our fault, and there is nothing wrong with us.

As a little girl, I was becoming strong, teaching myself how to survive the next traumatic event that would happen to me.

It's no wonder we become confused about who we are, what we should be doing, and how we should be acting. We become people pleasers without even knowing it, because we weren't taught to use our voice and tell people how we really feel.

If we were brave enough to try speaking out in the past, we may have gotten punished in some way—physically or emotionally. The adults in your life may have told you that you were crazy and what you were saying was not truth. These punishments and denials cause us to sink deeper into confusion. We wonder about our identity and we second-guess every decision.

I want to encourage you to stand in your truth because *memories* can be tricky. We remember certain parts of what happened, and we know that it did happen, even if we can't paint the full picture in our mind. If you are reading this and you know something happened to you, I want you to know you are not crazy for thinking what you are thinking. Talk to someone who understands how memories work, because if you talk to someone who doesn't understand, they will try to shut you down and shutting down is the last thing that you need when your mind is trying to process it and heal from the pain.

Do you find yourself in this process? These behaviors lead us to doubt our self and our perceptions. We weren't taught it was okay to say, "No" and as adults, we wonder why our life is now spinning out of control.

As we heal, we no longer have to pretend. We don't have to apologize any more for stuff we didn't do or that isn't our responsibility, and we no longer have to walk around with our heads down feeling ashamed if something triggers us.

We are entitled to our feelings, our reality, and our experiences. When you heal, you will be able to learn to trust again, to feel your feelings, and to talk about your experiences.

For many years I have lived with a lot of fear, never wanting to upset people. The little girl that I had become was how I operated for years—a scared little girl who was in hiding and afraid to come out and express herself. I often thought *if I did express how I really felt, what would people think of me. Will they like me? Will I be punished?* If you are ever around someone who apologizes for everything they do, they probably had a physically abusive or critical parent growing up or a parent who struggled with an addiction.

Each of us must find our voice or we will never face our fear as an adult. When the little girl inside me started to speak up, I told my therapist what I really wanted to say to my abusers about what I experienced, including rejection, abuse, neglect, and sexual abuse.

When I found my voice, I let all my feelings come to surface. For example, my therapist gave me permission to say everything I wanted to say to my abusers, even a few choice words, if you know what I mean. And these aren't words that would be used in religious settings. I told the people who hurt me how I really felt, even though they were not in front of me. I let it all out. I said what they did to me was disgusting, and they should be ashamed of themselves. I even told my earthly father that what he did to me, he will never do it again.

I would like to encourage you to find a therapist or someone else who has gone through their healing and abuse issues to talk to.

What would you really want to say to your abusers? Even if it is family, get in touch with your true feelings, so you can face your fear and pain and move on.

I needed to deal with my pain because it was affecting every area of my life. Whenever I started a new job I told myself to be that good little girl and everything will be okay. I promised myself that I was going to be perfect and do my job better than anyone. All I really wanted was for someone to validate all the brokenness that I was feeling inside. I worked so hard at all my jobs in hopes that I would be liked at work. In the end all the hard work left me feeling more defeated because my coworkers picked up on my weaknesses and insecurities and took advantage of my people-pleasing behaviors. They would say things to me that I knew were not right but once again I didn't want to upset anybody because I never wanted anybody mad at me or not to like me. This pattern followed me into many relationships until I learned who I really was, and I was no longer afraid to speak up and use my voice.

There is a difference between being nice and being a doormat. It's okay to love Jesus and not allow people to mistreat you.

Learn what your boundaries are. What are you willing to accept and not accept? Discover your values and never compromise. For instance, if you like to go to bed early, then don't allow people to show up at your house all hours of the night. If you enjoy a clean home, then talk with your family and explain that to them. Have people take their shoes off before they come into your home. What I am telling you may sound silly, but it's really not. People live with a lot of resentment because they don't know how to put healthy boundaries in place. When you don't know how to stand up for yourself, you can get very sick on the inside because you are holding all that bitterness in, and you are not saying what you really want to say.

I can remember in my early twenties I bought some really cool red couches, and it took a lot of my hard-working money to get them. Then I had some visitors come over with their children, and the children jumped all over my new couches. I was not able to enjoy their company because I didn't know how to tell them to stop. I can remember how upset I was and after they left, I cried my eyes out. Then when they wanted to come over again, I avoided them—because I didn't know how to speak up for myself.

I was still fearful of speaking my truth because I didn't want to feel the sting of rejection. Learning how to tell someone how you really feel is a two-process step. First you have to heal that fearful little child inside of you, and second you find the courage and strength to say how you are really feeling whether people like you or not. Here my famous saying again, "mean what you say, say what you mean." I know I've already shared this in a previous chapter but sometimes we need to keep hearing something over and over to let it sink in.

People who grow up in addiction and abuse usually struggle with what I have been describing. We become affected by the family's dysfunction until we recover from it. If we are not willing to get the help we need, we will spend most of our lives living with the effects of growing up in a dysfunctional home.

I wasted many years and my anxiety was high. I never felt joy. Some of these old behaviors still try to control my life today, but I have people who I can call—people who will help me check my motives and make sure my thinking and actions are clear. When we are learning to change and we've been traumatized from abuse or addiction, it's important to talk with someone who understands how addiction affects the entire family.

Trauma Shatters One's Identity

No matter how much time has passed, trauma stays in your body and mind. I hope my story helps people understand some of the things they may have experienced.

Later in life when I started to heal from trauma, and I was able to start relaxing on the inside (*what I mean is I started to feel safe*), I could feel tension leaving my body. Next thing you know is I could feel my digestive track start to relax and let go of stress. What most people don't realize is that we hold most of our emotions in the gut. That is why people say I get butterflies in my stomach. The more that I went through the process of healing the trauma in my body my digestive system healed, and I was off all medicines like laxatives and acid reflux meds and relieved of pain in my stomach.

Trauma affects us in so many ways. Healing has to start from the inside out. Too often we are so focused on the outside appearance. I get it. I did that, too. I struggled for years until I hit bottom and finally surrendered and accepted the fact that I needed a lot of help.

During my teenage years, I tried to fit in with different crowds. There was a season I started hanging around only African American kids in middle school, and I started talking in the same accent they used and put grease in my hair with braids. Every group I tried fitting into, I adapted. I was not myself. I did not have my unique identity. Later on in middle school when I was jumped into a Hispanic gang. I started wearing baggy clothes like gang members did and dressing like a boy. Then a few years later in high school, I met a very pretty blonde girl, and we became friends. I dreamed what it would be like to look like her. I asked her if she would help me find an outfit for school and do my hair. We ended up dressing up for a dance and dressing alike and took pictures together, but it didn't last very long. I felt very uncomfortable with a little makeup on and my hair done. I was so full of self-hate that I didn't feel worthy to dress in this way.

Do you see the pattern here? How I moved from group to group because I was confused in my own identity. I was not given a solid foundation to build on and when we are raised in a broken home and addiction, we lack self-confidence.

But I would like you to know that after my healing, there was such joy in learning who I really was underneath all the pain. I started to enjoy the simple activities of life, like getting dressed or going shopping because I was going to buy what I liked and dress how I wanted to. In my discovery of becoming my true self, I have developed a unique style. I still might ask a friend when we are out shopping if they like what I am buying, but secretly whether they like it or not, I will still buy it for myself. Today I mix my style with a little bit of classy and a little bit of the tomboy look. This brings me peace of knowing I am not forgetting where I came from, but also enjoy my new-found confidence.

Afraid to Be Me

When we were born we were created in the image of God, and then something traumatic happens in our life, like neglect or abuse, which crushes our self-image and we can no longer see ourselves the way God wants us to. We now view ourselves through the lens of our wounded soul.

I love what this Bible scripture says, "And yet, O Lord, you are our Father. We are the clay, and you are the potter. *We all are formed by your hand*" (Isaiah 64:8 NLT).

We were all made unique in the image of God. Not one of us is supposed to look identical to another person. Yes, we might resemble our parents or take after them in some way, but we were all created differently. And I believe in order to find out what that uniqueness is, we must spend time with him and in his Word. He helps us gain confidence and peace in who we really are. Also, I love that this scripture addresses that God is our Father because so many of us grow up without a father figure and that absence will really break a person's identity. I am going to be talking more about that in the next chapter, and I am really excited about it, because the pain and confusion that I felt in this area has taught me so much.

When we fall underneath the umbrella of trauma, we see ourselves through all of our experiences and pain. All it takes is just one traumatic experience to leave us with a distorted image of ourselves. Lies become attached to the experience, and when the pain is too much, we find ways to try to block out the memory or numb the pain. This is why trauma stays hidden for so long.

The keys to freedom take work with a lot of courage to face the past, vulnerability, and the willingness to shed tears and feel the anger. We have to learn to understand we no longer need the approval of people or for people to love us. We have to start owning who we really are and what we want to be. At first this freedom will be hard because we have always tried to get the approval and love from those who are the closest to us like our parents, caregivers, or loved ones.

In this season we need to draw close to God and learn about his character, so often we can think that God is angry with us because we feel like he could have prevented our trauma. But understand we live in a world with hurting and broken people. The more that we can understand

God's thoughts towards us and how much he loves us, the easier it will be to walk into our true identity.

When we learn about God and His character, we learn that He is a loving God. We learn that He created all of us to be different. When I started reading the Bible and praying to God, it helped me understand that I should only care about how God thinks of me and make sure my heart and thoughts were right with Him.

This world and the people in it can put high expectations on us. Expecting us to look and act perfect at all times—that is just unrealistic. Not only that, it will make you feel confused. When we've experienced abuse or neglect we are so quick to try to please everyone, but when we learn that we are enough and loved just the way we are, we will be able to get free from this pattern.

But remember we need God to show us the truth with the help of a therapist and a mentor to work hand-in-hand in our life. When we start to change, we need someone validating that what we are doing is right and our thinking is right.

This is what the Bible says about spending time with God, Jesus said it this way, "*But first and most importantly* seek (aim at, strive after) His kingdom and His righteousness...and *all these things will be given to you also*" (Matthew 6:33 AMP Emphasis Mine).

It sounds pretty simple doesn't it? Put God first; then all the rest will be given to you. But it takes self-discipline and hard work on your end. You will have to put in the effort daily of renewing your mind. It's not just going to happen for you, you have to be willing to do the work of changing old behaviors, emotions, and patterns. It might even take changing your current surroundings, because sometimes we need to step away from what is familiar.

When I started to come out of my shell, it was fun and kind of scary at the same time. One of the changes I noticed right away was my relationship with certain friends. Some chose to stay, and some chose to leave. It was hard and painful at first, but looking back now I am so glad I no longer have some of those friends, because it has given me space and more freedom to grow into my true identity.

I had to gain confidence and learn it was okay to have fun and not be so serious all the time. The more that you heal and find the peace within the more you will be able to enjoy your life.

I know all these changes may sound too basic, but each small change adds up to becoming something great and that is becoming the real *you*!

reflection

In this chapter we explored our true identity. Where do you feel you are in this process? Are you okay with using your voice when necessary? Think about where you are and write your honest thoughts in your journal.

"Looking at the truth may be difficult when you are hurting, but actually it is the only way to get free."

1. What do you feel is holding you back from being who you really want to be? What are some action steps you can take to help you break free from this stronghold?

2. What do you think your life would be like if you stopped people-pleasing and let go of caring what people think about you?

3. Are there some people in your life that you need to let go? Spend some time praying about this? Who does God bring to your mind?

prayer

Dear God,
Please help me to let go of the fear of man, and help me to identify
the lies that are keeping me stuck in not growing into my full
potential. I am ready to be who you created me to be, which is a
loving person who is confident in your own identity.
In Jesus' name I pray. Amen.

scripture

"See how very much our Father loves us, for he calls us his children, and that is what we are! But the people who belong to this world don't recognize that we are God's children because they don't know him" (1 John 3:1 NLT).

"You made all the delicate, inner parts of my body and knit me together in my mother's womb. Thank you for making me so wonderfully complex!" (Psalm 139:13-14 NLT).

"Being confident of this, that he who began a good work in you will carry it on to completion until the day of Christ Jesus" (Philippians 1:6 NLT).

CHAPTER 9

Transformed by the father's love

*Many of us had (or still have) earthly dads who missed the mark
in countless ways. Maybe their lives were affected by abuse and
neglect from their fathers, and they didn't know how to show
love and compassion. The void that comes with the lack of a
father's love sets us up for a lifetime of hardship and failure until
that wound is addressed.*

Men and women cope with their father wounds in different ways. Most men become workaholics or struggle with an addiction, while most women—me included—will marry men who subconsciously remind them of their father in some way. On some mysterious level we hardly acknowledge that we feel unworthy to be with someone who would treat us well. Another common factor among women who have father wounds is the struggle with eating disorders—overeating or under eating.

The father wound runs deep into the pit of our souls. Each person needs the blessings and affirmation of a father, and when we don't receive it, we spend the rest of our lives trying to somehow fill that vacuum.

I am living proof that you don't have to live that way anymore—chasing the approval of one man. Your Father in Heaven already approves of you and offers you His perfect love. God can and will restore to you what was stolen if you are willing to open your heart to His healing and forgiveness. You, too, can be transformed by a Father's love!

Memories of my Dad

My husband and I took a trip to Las Vegas in the summer of 2018 with our ten-year-old son. I wanted to show my husband and son where I grew up as a child and what schools I attended. I also got to visit my spiritual mom, who is now 75 years old. She holds a special spot in my heart and still lives in Las Vegas. In this book I often write about what she has taught me. She has played a huge part in my healing process. She loved me even when I didn't know how to love myself, and she often spoke these words to me: "One day you will learn that you are already enough." It has taken almost ten years, but now I believe those words.

During our trip to Las Vegas, my husband and son wanted to visit a few places they wanted to check off their bucket list. One place was Counts Kustom, a famous hot rod and chopper customization and restoration shop in the heart of Las Vegas. This shop also has a reality TV series on the History Channel, which my husband and son love watching together. The next place they wanted to visit was the world-famous Gold & Silver Pawn Shop in downtown Las Vegas, home of the TV hit show *Pawn Stars,* which we watch quite frequently in our home. When we arrived at the pawn shop, there was a line to get in. The temperature was around 110 degrees, so I am grateful our wait wasn't much longer than ten minutes. As we were standing outside, I saw a tall building out the corner of my eye, sitting kitty-corner from where we were standing. This building looked familiar to me.

After we left the pawn shop, I asked my husband if I could drive the rental car around the block because I couldn't get that building out of my head. I wanted to drive as close as possible to the building and the neighborhood to see why that atmosphere felt so familiar. As I drove I noticed we were in an older part of Las Vegas—most buildings in this particular area looked shabby and worn down. You could find some of the older casinos like Fremont there. I passed Stewart Avenue, and as I looked down the street, I remembered an older building that was on the corner. That was where I attended my first recovery meeting at the age of twenty-four.

The memories flooded back. When I walked into my first recovery meeting, I was in a desperate state. A week prior to that first meeting, I was contemplating suicide. This meeting is where I met my spiritual mom. In a recovery program, you start to work on your healing and recovery journey. The person is called your sponsor, but it didn't take long for the relationship between my spiritual mom and me to become more like a mother-daughter relationship. Almost twenty years later our relationship is still strong, even though I left Las Vegas in 2004 and relocated to Michigan. With God's provision, I have been able to go visit her a few times.

As I made my way around the block, I spotted that tall building that looked so familiar to me. It was the Clark County Detention Center—the jail for Las Vegas, Nevada. This struck me as ironic. When I was my son's age going into the sixth grade, I used to have to go to this building to visit my dad. He was locked up there for a year until he was sent to prison for another ten years. It's a very tall building with many small windows. When visitation was over with my dad, he would tell us kids to stand on the street corner and look for him and wave. There was always somebody in the window waving back to us, and to be honest, I'm not sure if it was my dad or somebody else. There were a lot of windows, and he wasn't the only one waving and standing in the window. It felt like he was probably on the twenty-second floor, because I remember having to look way up.

Memories are like falling dominoes; one leads to another.

Fast forward with me for a minute from all these old memories I was having while in Las Vegas to the fall of 2016 when I was attending my father's funeral on my fortieth birthday—October 27.

A few weeks prior my father was placed in hospice, and my siblings and I took turns going to visit or stay with him.

On a few nights, I slept in his room with him. I don't know if it was much sleep because all they had in the room was a regular sitting chair, not a recliner chair. It really didn't matter to me at the moment, I just wanted to spend some time with him.

I had waited my whole life for the opportunity to spend quality time with him, but we just couldn't find the right time, and we just didn't know how to make it happen, due to our brokenness. He was still struggling with his addiction and childhood trauma, and I was trying to heal from the many wounds from my childhood growing up with trauma, neglect, addiction, and abuse.

My father was raised by two parents who were, from what I hear, extremely abusive, especially his father. His father was an alcoholic and did some horrible things to my father. My father had to learn how to take care of himself as young as the age of eight, by eating out of a dumpster and keeping himself warm in the middle of winter when my grandfather would lock him out of the house. He was locked up in juvenile detention for the first time as early as thirteen years old. He was in and out of boys' homes most of his teenage life.

He had lived in a beat-up old farmhouse. It needed a lot of work, but it was very spacious. He kept most of his belongings in a little kitchen area. Instead of a dining table in the kitchen, he had his bed, a small old TV, and a place to hang a few of his clothes. I often wondered why he slept in the kitchen when there was a bedroom right down the hall. My husband pointed out something to me one day. My father was locked up most of his life as a child and an adult. He was in prison a few times, in jail, mental institutions, and boys' homes as a young boy and teenager. He was also homeless. So his whole life he was used to having all his belongings in one room. He was used to being confined. It made him feel safe. But he really wasn't safe at all.

Two Wounded Souls

Two wounded people, such as my dad and me, really can't have a healthy relationship because they don't know how. We put too many expectations on the other person to meet our needs when they themselves are hurting, lost, and confused.

During the few days I stayed at the hospital with my dad, I watched him suffer as fluid filled his stomach, a side-effect from the cancer in his body. One night he woke up and needed to use the restroom. I called the nurse in to help me assist him. It took two of us to help him stand up. The young female nurse and myself struggled to help him up because my father was 6 foot 3 with a large frame. Even though he was loopy because of being on morphine and he could barely stand, he was still trying to function by using the restroom. That night I saw a part of him I've never seen before; he was shy when the nurse and I tried to help him pull down his pants.

After he finished trying to use the restroom which was futile because he could barely sit, and his body was already shutting down, the nurse and I helped him lay back down in his bed. I then sat next to him on his bed, and he was trying to look at me, but it was hard for him to focus. He stared at my face. Then as he dialed in to see my face, he kept nodding his head. At this point he couldn't get any words out, and all I could do was grab hold of what I believed he was trying to say to me. My heart still wanted something from him.

My dad and I never really had a close relationship, even though I desired it my whole life. After I moved out on my own, I struggled with my own addictions and an eating disorder for a while. When I found recovery, I had to stay away from him in order to protect myself from reverting to the things I used to do to numb my pain. Being around all the addiction and dysfunction in my family brought too much pain to my soul, especially when I was trying to heal and recover. Oddly enough this doesn't mean I didn't miss all of them and the dysfunction.

This process is important to notice, because sometimes in order to heal you have to give yourself the freedom to put some space between you and the other parties that caused a lot of your wounds. Being around a wound-maker, even someone you love, can trigger you to run back to the unhealthy addictions that once helped you cope with your pain.

Going back to that moment with my dad sitting on the bed, he kept looking at me and nodding his head. What came to me so strongly was that my dad was shocked to see me there. Since we didn't see each other that much, he probably thought I would be the last one to be sitting by his side at the hospital.

I wasn't one of his children who was usually around much. I did stay in contact by phone like once a month and maybe visited him a few times a year. Some of my other siblings were okay with having a few beers with him. But I could no longer put myself in situations where I could possibly be wounded further or give him the opportunity to say something that would hurt me deeply. My wounds were still seeping and trying to heal, yet my heart still wanted something from him. Does your heart still long for something that your dad could never give you?

People with good relationships with their fathers often don't understand the depth of someone else's father wound. If you were hurt, abused, neglected, abandoned, or ignored by your father, you may feel misunderstood and alone. I am right here with you, understanding your broken heart and encouraging you to press on through your healing journey. That effort to heal is why I explain what it took for me to heal and be free from the pain of the relationship with my father, which caused so many other issues. I also feel it's important for others to hear my story, because my father and I didn't have a radical story of redemption. I had to learn to accept my father for who he was. I had to understand that I was never going to get what my soul deeply longed for from him.

Have you learned to accept your father the way he really is or was? Can you come to terms with the fact that you may never get what you long for from him? I want to help you deal in reality—to fully accept what is and what was.

The Difference Between Understandable and Acceptable Behavior

When the father figure in your life is abusive or absent, it leaves a deep emotional scar that needs to be healed for you to see yourself as you really are. My identity was distorted because I didn't feel like my earthly father loved me. He called me filthy names and abused me. At a young age I felt broken and like I wanted to die. In my recovery journey of healing I had to work through this pain with people who reminded me that I am lovable and his treatment toward me wasn't my fault.

Because someone else's pain is understandable doesn't mean that their behavior is acceptable. You may look at your dad's life, his painful past, and the abusive, neglectful way his caregivers treated him, and it might make sense why he turned into the man he did. But that doesn't mean how he treated you was okay. You can forgive someone and still know you deserved far better treatment.

When my father was fixated on my face on his deathbed, I looked deep into his eyes. "Yes, it's me, Dad. Your daughter Paula. I want you to know that there is nothing you have done to me that has ever made me stop loving you." I rubbed my hand through his coarse hair, which I honestly think was the first time in my entire life I'd ever touched him in that way. With tears dripping down my cheeks, I leaned in and kissed his clammy forehead.

I knew this was it. This was going to be the last time I saw my dad here on earth, breathing, alive. I believe God set up this moment for me, so I could be released from anything toxic that might still be inside of me—such as unforgiveness. It gave me such freedom to know that God had healed me enough to love this man who didn't deserve it. I wanted peace for him and myself and I wanted him to know how much I loved him.

That night I reached for my iPhone and snapped a few pictures of my hand holding his. It was a moment I never wanted to forget.

The next night my father took his last breath. My brother was with him, and he describes my father letting out a roar when he left this earth. That sounds about right for him, since he was such a fighter in all areas of his life.

As I repeatedly have said in these pages, wounded people will use food or substances or relationships to numb the pain of past abuse or neglect. If trauma is not treated it can also cause mental illness. My father was diagnosed with bipolar disorder and schizophrenia. When he slept, he would scream in his sleep like he was fighting with someone.

My constant prayer for my father was that he would find peace and healing in his heart. I believe when he left this earth, he found both.

The questions I often ask myself—and you may ask yourself as well—are these:

How can you love someone so much yet have feared him your whole life?

How can you have a profound attachment to someone you never really knew?

The best way I know to describe my relationship with my earthly father is, I longed for his love and attention, but I didn't dare ask him for it.

We never knew what we were going to get from him. He was a man suffering and wrestling with his unique demons from his childhood trauma. And so, he caused his children to suffer.

Understandable, yet not acceptable.

Before I end this chapter, I will transition into what helped me to heal, but before I do so I want to say this: just because your parents or caregivers were abused doesn't give them the right to do it to you. But unfortunately, until someone is strong enough to break the cycle, this pattern of abuse and dysfunction usually continues.

Allowing God to Bring Our Deep Wounds to the Surface

How do we begin to break the chains of the past? We must start allowing God to uncover our old wounds and bring them to the surface so they can be healed. Any pain which is denied and buried can never be healed.

My first steps to restoration were when I could grasp the fact that my father was a sick man. He couldn't give me what he didn't have.

It's so simple but true. Our fathers can't give us what they don't have. If they are wounded, they will wound us.

How do you grasp the truth about your parent? There are many levels of the process, beginning with a brutally honest look at your father (mother, brother, sister, uncle …) and how he/they treated you. You may get angry at what happened to you. It was unacceptable and you deserved to be adored, kept safe, paid attention to, and lavishly loved. But you were not.

Often guilt comes along with this process. I wondered if I should've done more or tried harder. But when I examined my heart, I know I did all I could have done to try to have a relationship with my father. I know in my heart I forgave him, but I still had to keep him at a distance. This process was not only important to follow with my father but also with my mother. When each one passed away, a little guilt crept in. *You should've spent more time with them*, the voices accused.

But because of my personal healing, I know I did the right thing by keeping away—keeping myself safe.

Just as you would never allow your children to be near toxic fumes that could harm them, you, as a wounded adult, also need to stay away from toxic relationships.

We need time and space to sort through our personal issues. I was so confused with all my behaviors, like cutting my body and binge eating and purging. I needed to be surrounded by healthy, life-giving people who understood the healing process. I wanted the space to dissect all these behaviors that were controlling me. I needed time to heal and work on creating healthier habits instead of self-harming.

Learning to accept that my father was never going to be able to give me what I was longing for was a crucial lesson. The experience will be challenging for you, too.

For me, I needed to take the time to learn about the Heavenly Father, how he loved me, cared for me, and accepted me. I needed time to learn I was lovable even though my parents couldn't express love to me.

I began to listen to my real Father, the one who crafted me with His two hands and said I was His workmanship. I listened to Him tell me I was okay. I was lovable. That I was enough. That I no longer needed to strive or perform or contort myself into somebody else.

In the beginning, people in my recovery program, like my spiritual mom, told me these truths. Then I quieted my mind enough to learn about the character of God—the God who forgives our sins and who loves us unconditionally. The more I healed and learned what was causing my pain, I knew I needed a new daddy to step in, so I opened myself up to my Creator, Abba Father in heaven.

I learned to talk to God about every hurt in my heart and every dark sin I was still struggling with. I learned that it is God who heals. Only He is able to reach into my heart and your heart and perform the unexplainable and miraculous!

Will you take the first step and ask God to be your Father? Allow Him to touch the damaged, dark parts of your heart. Tell Him everything, because He knows already, and He longs to bind up your wounds and bring you healing.

Believe what God's word says about you—you are His beloved child. You are accepted, loved, forgiven, cared for, and more precious than gold and rubies. These life-giving messages will ultimately replace the old, damaging self-talk. And remember we believe this new message by faith not by feelings. Learning how much He loves you will be a daily challenge. Sometimes you will vacillate and feel defeated and hopeless. But then you get up, brush yourself off, and grab hold of God's love, His promises, and His purpose for you. He will give you the strength and boldness to move forward. God the Father will transform you with his love.

reflection

You can't heal a wound by denying it's not there. Yet many of us try. We don't want to feel our hurts. We don't want to revisit painful memories. So, we continue to deny them. Maybe we stay busy by overworking or hiding behind our addiction. Maybe we distract ourselves with entertainment or other compulsions like perfectionism or overeating or staying angry and spewing rage on people. We don't want to cry or feel the pain, so we repress it.

Here are a few thoughts about father wounds and trauma:

Clinical research strongly suggests that childhood trauma and neglect are stored in the tissues of the children. Emotional and physical trauma does not go away without an effort to address the original cause.

127

Tools we can use to help us recover from childhood trauma are recovery programs, mentors who have healed from past experiences of brokenness, or trauma therapists. Recovery is not easy. It often takes considerable effort, and it's not a journey meant to be walked alone. God brings people to walk with us.

The process of recovery involves real work and determination that pays dividends beyond our expectations. If we are willing to stay on this recovery journey, if we trust the process and promises of God, our bodies can release the stored trauma, which brings us true relief physically, mentally, and spiritually.

Abuse by authority figures, such as our fathers, in childhood sets us up to be on guard as adults regarding other authority figures.

Fear of authority figures in our adult life can add unnecessary stress when old fears get triggered. As children, many of us were constantly on guard in case we displeased our parent or needed to find a hiding place when danger was present.

To gain control over our lives, when we interact with someone in authority, we can do a quick internal check. Are we feeling fearful, angry, resentful, or timid? Are we putting our alcoholic or abusive parent's face on this person? This is the time to get centered and remind yourself you are safe now.

1. Did you have a relationship with your earthly father? Was he a part of your younger life? Write about him in a journal. If he was absent in some way, how did it make you feel, then and now?

2. What are your memories of your earthly father? If you have none, describe the feelings attached to that empty place in your life.

3. Ask God to show you damaged feelings regarding your father that need healing. What feelings is He showing you?

prayer

Dear God,
I feel this father wound area is holding me back in my life and I
am not sure where to begin to get to a place where I trust you with
all my heart and all my pain. I want to surrender my dysfunctional
ways and coping mechanisms to you. I ask you now to come into
my heart and expose any father or mother wounds and help me
recognize my false beliefs and destructive patterns.
In Jesus' name I pray. Amen.

scriptures

"But to all who believed him and accepted him, he gave the right to become children of God" (John 1:12 NLT).

"So you have not received a spirit that makes you fearful slaves. Instead, you received God's Spirit when he adopted you as his own children. Now we call him, 'Abba, Father.' For his Spirit joins with our spirit to affirm that we are God's children. And since we are his children, we are his heirs. In fact, together with Christ we are heirs of God's glory. But if we are to share his glory, we must also share his suffering. Yet what we suffer now is nothing compared to the glory he will reveal to us later" (Romans 8:15–18 NLT).

"And yet, O Lord, you are our Father. We are the clay, and you are the potter. We are all formed by your hand" (Isaiah 64:8 NLT).

"And I will be your Father, and you will be my sons and daughters, says the Lord Almighty" (2 Corinthians 6:18 NLT).

CHAPTER 10

Stepping into wholeness

*God desires for you to be free from bondage. He understands when
you are tired of trying to do what's right, and you want to give up
and go back to old ways. All He requires of you is to continue to
trust Him and be patient with yourself as He rebuilds your life.*

Learning a whole new way of living is not easy. Believe me, I get it.
It was extremely hard for me to break free from years of addiction,
abuse, and family dysfunction. There have been many times I have found
myself feeling guilty for searching for a better way to live. I had settled
way too long with the concept this was how my life was suppose to be.
The seeds that were planted into my life at a very young age said that life
is full of crisis and dysfunction, and life should be hard.

There could have been no way for me to embrace the healing process
until I was ready to look at my life experience and put a voice to it. I had
to get to the point where I could say this is what happened to me. For too
long I was hiding behind suppressed memories from childhood trauma.

The other day when I sat down to read my Bible a piece of paper fell
out. What was written on it reminded me how far I have come. The lines
on the paper were pretty faded because I wrote it more than three years
ago. I would like to share a part of it with you. Because I want you to
know that I understand what it's like to be miserable, stuck in patterns,
mindsets, and relationships that are unhealthy, but yet, long to be free at
the same time.

Dear Jesus, I'm tired. I don't want to live like this anymore. My body is sick from all the binge eating. Please show me the mental blocks that are stopping me from getting free from self-destructive behaviors and my eating disorder? Expose the lies that I am being controlled by and give me the memories I need to heal from so I can become whole in you.

I often wonder where my life would be today if I had never decided to do the work of healing from trauma. I know that I would not be here writing this book or be able to support other people who are fighting the same battles I fought. I am actually struggling as I write this chapter because I don't want to repeat the information I have already shared with you but at the same time I know I need to keep speaking powerful truth. People need to hear truth over and over again in order to allow it to sink in. I am going to do my best to explain what it cost me to walk into freedom. People look at my life today and see how happy I am with an amazing husband, nice car, and beautiful home, they often treat me differently, but they have no idea what it took to get here.

So many times I meet people who want to get free but they are not willing to keep fighting and trying different paths until they find their answer. I do believe with all my heart Jesus is the ultimate deliverer and healer but He will use other resources and people to assist you on your journey to recovery.

I spent many nights by myself crying in bed. Up all night with anxiety gripping my chest. Left alone in an emergency room as I miscarried a baby because the father beat me. Giving birth to a baby at 15 years old while my dad was in prison and my mom was no where to be found because of her addiction. Trying to survive while taking care of my baby and little brother while there was no food in the house or parental supervision.

I want you to understand years and years of trauma take time to heal. I did not trust anybody for a very long time. I learned how to be a survivor and I was going to take care of myself no matter the cost. In my teen years I became a thief in order to clothe and feed myself, my son, and my little brother.

I'm going to pause right here and ask God to minister to your heart as you continue reading. My hope is that I tap into something that has been holding you back.

Are you truly ready to do what it takes to step into wholeness?

I have grieved too many people in my life who have died early from violence or drug overdose, or who are sitting in prison. I don't want you to be one of them. Not only do I want a different life for you, but I know that is God's plan for you, too.

It doesn't matter what you witnessed growing up. You can change the cycle of addiction and dysfunction and live a different life if you choose to take the journey into wholeness.

Perfection is an Illusion

One of the biggest myths I feel so many people are striving for is perfection. Yes, perfection. I think so many of us are working hard to get to this goal that doesn't even exist.

When I was so broken I use to look at people lives and compare my life all the time. I use to think that people who dressed really nice must have a really good life or if I saw a beautiful woman married to a handsome guy I would think to myself they must have a good relationship. It wasn't until I went through my journey of healing and started to share my story that I found out pretty quick that was far from the truth for most people. Actually I learned there are a lot of people who look happy on the outside but they are struggling with the same pain I've faced.

I love this quote from Brenè Brown, "Want to be happy? Stop trying to be perfect."

When we are working on becoming whole we need to understand up front that trying to strive to be *perfect* is a big fat lie, and no one will ever achieve it. The Bible tells us that on earth there will be many trials and we will face pain and sorrow. And no one on this earth is perfect or do they have a perfect life. Every person has some sort of issue or dysfunction he or she is trying to sort through.

To be honest, as I type this chapter I can still get tripped up with old behaviors or ways of thinking. "Why?" you might ask. Because old patterns of thinking and past behaviors take time to heal.

Walking into wholeness or freedom doesn't mean you won't have struggles. Actually to be free we need to expose the lie of perfection and the need to look as if we have it all together—as if having no problems will be the way to find freedom and true happiness.

Perfection is a lie.

I spent years obsessing over how I looked, how clean my house was, and making sure my children never acted out like normal children do. I walked through my struggles the hard way, putting a lot of unnecessary pressure on myself. I beat myself up about my missteps until I understood that I will never be perfect or nor do I ever want to be. Actually, people who act like they have it all together make me nervous if I am around them for too long. My ultimate goal in life is to be authentic with people, not try to prove that I am perfect.

In the next few weeks I will be 43 years old, and I am so grateful today I can put a pair of jeans on with a t-shirt and throw my messy hair in a bun and head out the door. Before when I was hiding behind my wounds I would have never done this. I've practiced over the years positive affirmations to combat all the negative beliefs.

I want to empower you to never wait to love yourself until you are perfect and have no more problems. You might be waiting for the rest of your life. I spent a lot of years wondering what it would be like to be like someone else, have their life, and even look like them. I didn't start to find peace until I fully learned to love and embrace myself, all of me, even my story.

It's Okay To Put Yourself First

Mental confinement is the mindset that keeps us trapped. Pastor Steven Furtick from Elevation Church defines this as head chatter. Breaking free from the thought processes we've had for years is not an easy process. Actually, it's going to take work. At first it may feel scary to start to think differently and act differently from all you have ever known your whole life.

When I used to feel this way, I thought that I was not making any progress, but every time I had a day of struggling in my identity or emotions, I always came back stronger. For instance, if I said yes to something I really didn't want to do, the next day I would find the strength to pick up the phone and back out of it. This may not sound like a person of integrity, but I was so tired of doing things I did not really want to do. Especially when I was in the season of changing and discovering who I really was. I did not need to put myself in a place or position where I was going to be comparing myself to other people, places, or things.

There was a season where I had to keep myself protected from certain situations. Things that were going to drain me because I didn't really want to be there in the first place, if you find yourself dreading to do or go somewhere listen to your gut or inner voice. How do you really feel about the situation? Give yourself permission to be true to what you really want and desire.

I'm going to share an example of a time I had to put a boundary in place and it was not easy. During my season of being a single mom, I had a few friends from church who always wanted me to go out for dinner and drinks on the weekend. They were very good at making it sound like we were going to have fun, and they were good at saying things that would make me feel guilty for not going, "Let's go out tonight; I haven't seen you in so long. Just let your older kids babysit your toddler."

I always felt trapped. *How am I going to tell them no this time? I knew I really didn't have the money to go, and I didn't want to leave my children home alone.* I couldn't figure out how to say no so I said, "Sure, I'll meet you there."

After the night was over I stayed awake, wrestling with a conviction that I shouldn't have gone with them. I knew I would be tired the next day and that my children needed me. Not to mention I'd spent grocery and gas money that I will need for the next few weeks.

I was still fighting the battle of people pleasing and wanting everybody to like me. I was still wrestling with the new life I wanted. I really wanted peace, calm, and to love myself and honor God. Yet I said yes to them.

This kind of scenario had to happen to me a handful more times until I finally got fed up and found the strength to tell both of my friends that I am a single mom and my kids need me and if they can't respect that then I guess we can't be friends anymore.

It was scary to do this as first but the moment I took action is when I felt strong and better about myself. I finally got to a point to do what was right for my children and me.

Boundaries are something we put in place to keep us safe and protect our environment. It's like putting up a wall to keep the good in and the bad out. One thing to remember is when you start establishing healthy boundaries people will not be happy with them.

Waking up to a new identity

I started to value who I was as a person and gave myself permission to put my healing first.

Self-acceptance and self-love, I believe, are the keys to the healing process. Learning to accept yourself—even the details you dislike about yourself.

When you are going through a process of change, it's hard to see all the baby steps that add up to positive change. I hope that what I share with you lights a spark inside of you and that you will never give up on yourself, your freedom, and healing journey. Life gets better when we do what is required of us to become healthy individuals. A healthy soul helps us be less dependent on people, places, and things that often fail us in the long run.

If you are ready to step into wholeness and all that God has for you, ask yourself if your friends and your surroundings are truly supporting your desires?

I want to stress the importance of asking for help and having those few friends that will hold you accountable and will be there for you in every season. Even the dark seasons. I have few select friends I can call on speed dial and say, "this girl needs prayer."

For the longest time I didn't feel worthy to live a life of joy, peace, and abundance. These feelings were because of all the self-hate I had toward myself. I hated who I was and who I had become. It was because I was taught to hate myself through years of rejection and abandonment by those who I wanted to love me.

After I married my husband, my eyes were open in so many ways. I believe God brought him to me because God knew he would be able to handle the healing I would be going through. After living with him for some time I witnessed how he handled situations in a calm manner. If we disagreed, he talked through the disagreement. I was ready to scream, kick, fight, and run away. I didn't know that when you are in a relationship with someone you can actually talk things through instead of shutting down or running away. My husband was consistent in his behavior, and I started to desire what he had.

The life that I came from I was used to accepting whatever would happen to me. My nights use to be gripped with fear until my husband taught me what a safe environment should be like.

The other day I had an old flash back, and it was hard for to believe it actually happened. When I was a young mom and in a full state of trauma that I didn't even realize at the time, we lived in a condo on government assistant section 8 housing. One night a gang member who was upset with the father of my three kids came to my house in the middle of the night. He was pointing a flashlight in my windows. I ducked down and tried to hide but I know he saw my children. Being scared and not knowing what to do I let him in. When he came in he had a very foul odor, and he pushed me to the ground. He stated he wanted to have sex with me because he was upset and said the father of my children had sex with a girl he was dating. Once again I found myself kick into survival mode. It was the thing I learned to do over and over in order to survive. He was intoxicated and passed out on my couch. The next morning I took him home. I remember putting my children in the car seat and right away he lit a joint. When he finally got out of the car I could not get away fast enough. Once again I was a victim of abuse reigniting my trauma.

As I look at my life now compared to where I came from, it's so hard to believe I survived.

I had to get used to living a life without all the dysfunction and chaos. My family and I still struggle, but it's not the constant drama that comes from growing up around addiction and abuse. Today when something happens, we talk about it, confront the problem, and we pray about it—then we take action. Before these kinds of disputes and issues would have been days of chaos and confusion and not knowing what to do next. After years of healing I have found peace enough to pray about everything (*okay most things*) and wait and see what God will do in my situation. I am very careful of who and what I allow in my life today.

We all have a story to tell, and it's for us to tell, if we choose to or not. I believe at some point we all experience some type of pain. Some people's lives are more painful than others. But it doesn't discount the fact that we all need healing. How do we do this? By accepting our story and being willing to go through the healing process. So often we try to protect ourselves from the truth because it's too painful, but facing the truth will set us free from our suffering.

When I was going through healing, I couldn't see or even think of the good things God had in store for my life. I am so glad I trusted the process. At first I didn't have the ability to see the beauty in my brokenness. But today I share my story with you, so you can see how God took my brokenness and used it for good—and He wants to do the same for you.

I've held on tight to my relationship with Jesus, His Word, other believers, and my recovery program. I've had to learn to surrender my life and my ways to Him. That means letting Him take over and show me what I need. There have been a lot of ups and downs, but all of it has played a huge part in my healing process. When I let Jesus into the depths of my heart and allowed Him to reveal all the pain that was hidden there, He took all my broken pieces and made them whole again. He has healed my heart. He has healed relationships. He has released me from my addictions. And even after a lifetime of being illiterate, He brought people in my life to teach me how to read. He has restored so much in my life and He wants to do this for you, too.

reflection

Are you ready to dream again? What dreams do you have that you thought you could never accomplish? Allow my story to inspire you to heal and dream again. My story is a picture of God fulfilling my biggest dreams of renewed identity, family, wholeness, and telling my story of transformation so others can heal. And most of all, living day to day with peace that only God can give.

1. What would it take for you to walk out your healing? Would you trust God to help you through this process?

2. What needs to be brought into the open and exposed so God can heal you? What causes you to go back to the dark places?

3.What changes in your life need to be put in place to start the journey to wholeness? What do you need to let go of? Make a list and don't hold back; write and pray about what comes to your memory.

prayer

Dear God,
Give me the courage to make the changes in my life that will bring
about wholeness. I am ready for a complete breakthrough. Even
though I don't know what that looks like, I'm ready to trust you and
your plan. I'm ready for you to remove all things and relationships
that are hindering my success and wholeness in this life here on
earth. I know I can't do this in my own strength, so help me to
spend time with you daily. In Jesus' name I pray. Amen.

scripture

"For I, the Lord, love justice. I hate robbery, and wrongdoing. I will faithfully reward my people for their suffering and make an everlasting covenant with them" (Isaiah 61:8 NLT).

serenity prayer

Reinhold Niebuhr (1892-1971)

God grant me the serenity
to accept the things I cannot change;
courage to change the things I can;
and wisdom to know the difference.

Living one day at a time;
enjoying one moment at a time;
accepting hardships as the pathway to peace;
taking, as He did, this sinful world
as it is, not as I would have it;
trusting that He will make all things right
if I surrender to His Will;
that I may be reasonably happy in this life
and supremely happy with Him
forever in the next.
Amen.[1]

---

1   https://www.beliefnet.com/prayers

about the author

*P*aula Jauch's life experience enables her speaking and writing to empower people from all walks of life. She shares her inspirational story all around the world through speaking and radio. Her goal is to carry this message to the forefront. She loves encouraging and motivating her audiences to live a life of freedom in Christ. She is a happily married mother of four and a proud Nana. In her spare time, you might find her at a favorite Mexican restaurant. Paula lives in West Michigan.

Paula's work experience led her to realize she needed healing from childhood trauma after growing up in abuse and addiction. After she graduated from an alternative education high school and had two children by age eighteen, her heart was drawn to jobs to help children like herself. She worked seven years at the Juvenile Court Schools in Las Vegas, Nevada, and five years at the Clark County Department of Family Services, as a juvenile service assistant, working with troubled teens. In 2004 she relocated to Terre Haute, Indiana, where she worked for two years at Gibault Inc., as a youth specialist, working with teen boy sex offenders. After leaving the Gibault home, she worked a few months at the Vigo County Courthouse as a bailiff, but decided to leave her job when it became uncomfortable, because her family name was well known in the court system.

What she learned through all of her work experience is that if these kids didn't get the proper help they needed, they would get involved in a gang, addicted to drugs or alcohol, land in prison, or even face death. Paula knew she was being called to take a step of faith and action and get the help she needed so she could help others who experienced similar childhoods.

Even though Paula's story and passion centers around youth, men and women of all ages will be inspired by her story of restoration. Connect with Paula www.paulajauch.com or follow her on Instagram, Facebook and Twitter @paulajauch.

Order Information

REDEMPTION PRESS

To order additional copies of this book, please visit
www.redemption-press.com.
Also available on Amazon.com and BarnesandNoble.com
Or by calling toll free 1-844-2REDEEM.

CPSIA information can be obtained
at www.ICGtesting.com
Printed in the USA
LVHW042238130123
737045LV00004B/668